Daily

LEAR
HOW TO LOVE

MW00582093

Dr. Ally & Jeremy Butrous

ISBN: 978-1-7332548-4-7
Ebook ISBN: 978-1-7332548-5-4
Publisher: Radiant Publishing

TABLE OF CONTENTS

ABOUT
THE AUTHORS

Very few books offer relationally empowering skills from two people who are actively in a relationship themselves. Dr. Ally and Jeremy Butrous bring their years of experience in the fields of counseling and psychology (Ally) and ministry (Jeremy). They have dedicated their lives to learning how to bring out the best in each other, and others around them. This book is based on real-life experiences and breakthroughs, as well as wisdom they personally practice daily to live their best relational life!

HOW TO USE
THIS BOOK

This devotional is a biblically-based guide to growing and improving your relational skills and your relationships! Over the years, we have discovered two core elements of improving relationships. These two principles apply to every relationship you will ever have. These core elements are openness and ownership. These cornerstones set our relationships up for success. Without them, our relationships are doomed to failure! This devotional is a dance between biblically-based principles that help us perfect our relationships and psychology. With this synergy, we will not only build with the relational king Jesus but practically apply real-life tools in our daily lives. The most important thing to remember is that we can change ourselves. As we change ourselves, we start relating to others differently, and they respond differently. There is so much hope as we build off of the truth we find in scripture. We pray that as you turn the pages of this book and apply these concepts, you will start to see the slow and steady change in your heart, life, and interactions with others.

Below you will find a breakdown of how to use this book and its relatable components.

Quote:

This is an invitation to see and glean from the perspectives of others! In 2 Corinthians 13:1, Paul reminds us that a matter is established by two or three witnesses. These quotes encourage us and provide wisdom gleaned from preachers and Christian authors, as well as leaders, athletes, historical figures, psychologists, and public figures. The quotes were chosen to inspire you. This journey is a journey we do not take alone, and it is important to have other voices that help us think about the topics in new and engaging ways!

Scripture:

2 Timothy 3:16 says, "All Scripture is inspired by God and is useful to teach us what is true and to make us realize what is wrong in our lives. It corrects us when we are wrong and teaches us to do what is right" (New Living Translation). A biblical basis is the foundation for this devotional. The vibrancy of life is gleaned from the life of Jesus. Throughout this devotional, you will be invited into scriptural stories and principles that become the foundation for each topic. The scriptural references in this book are in no way exhaustive, but are meant to be a launching pad for context and understanding. The reader is encouraged to go beyond the references of scripture and study the word of God, for in it you will find life and meaning.

Teaching:

Wisdom is brought to us by experience and revelation. Within each devotional topic, we are invited into a progressive understanding that breaks down real areas of opportunity we face each and every day. Real situations, behaviors, mindsets, and attitudes of the heart are brought forth in each teaching. We can process them together using the Word of God, proven stories of victory, revelation, and wisdom. As we learn and grow with timely teaching, we are fashioned into a person who is a better reflection of Jesus. Our perspective begins to change and our life follows down a path that leads us to thrive.

Prayer:

Seeing God's perspective in every situation brings us access to keys and knowledge that position us to be victorious in our day. God is our source of life and He understands our humanity more than we do. Who is more qualified to speak into our trials and tribulations than Jesus Himself? No one! He has the answers to our needs, wants, and desires. Prayer is not just about what we say, but listening for and receiving a response. Hebrews 4:16 says, "Let us then with confidence draw near to the throne of grace, that we may receive mercy and find grace to help in time of need" (English Standard Version). As we pray, with His perspective in mind, we open up the Heavens of possibility over our lives. Let's see life through His eyes and run at the pace of His heart.

Reflection:

The reflection is a time to invite God into your thoughts, process the information, and allow the Holy Spirit to guide you. Romans 12:2 encourages us to "be transformed by the renewing of your mind." Renewing the mind doesn't happen by hearing only, but by hearing, reflecting, and applying that knowledge. Questions are given as starting points to consider how you might specifically apply this knowledge to transform your life. Not all need be answered, or answered in order. The most important thing is that you use this space to continue to process how you personally can expand your ability to intentionally love!

INTRODUCTION

God's love is unconditional, and He created us to thrive in an atmosphere of unconditional love, both in our relationships with Him and with others. As we understand God's priority for connection, we can't help but make this our priority as well. In fact, Jesus asked us to! His desire was for His people to love each other as He loved us (John 13:34).

It is abundantly hard to love if we have not first learned to receive love for ourselves, and give love to ourselves. When we sow avoidance, anger, annoyance, blame, or guilt toward ourselves, we reduce our ability to be an image-bearer of God. God loves Himself, but not in a narcissistic way. In our culture, if we say someone loves themselves, usually we mean they are so self-focused they do not share love, attention, interest, kindness, or encouragement toward others. God does not just think about Himself. Everything He does is to empower love, because God is love.

God also made a point to demonstrate that the Father, Son, and Spirit express love, trust, and work with each other. As that happens, greater love was shown through God to the world! His love for Himself multiplied His love toward others; it did not reduce it.

We were made in the image of God. If we speak poorly about ourselves, we reduce our ability to be our best self. God did not speak poorly about Himself. If God thought speaking and thinking poorly about ourselves was good and had a positive outcome, Jesus would have demonstrated this for us. He would have modeled negative speaking and self-judgment.

If we focus on our faults, we really demonstrate unhealthy self-focus that stops us from loving those around us in effective ways, and having the relationship outcomes we want. We do not bear the image of God when we refuse to align with His loving view of us, and instead align with our own negative judgments about ourselves. If this is a challenge, we invite you to stay tuned for our next book, Love Yourself, or find our course on radiantthoughts.com about biblical self-compassion.

This is not a book about that topic, but we mention it because one of the main reasons we see people try to change relationship dynamics and fail is because they have not first changed their relationship dynamic with themselves. If you find yourself getting stuck repeatedly, that might be the best place to start.

We assume, however, you are picking up this book because you desire to be in healthy, happy, safe and intimate relationships. For many people, relationships have been the exact opposite: unloving, unsafe, and distant. If we didn't have good relational models growing up, we probably haven't learned the tools of healthy relationships. We've probably learned other tools to try to manage the damage we are feeling in relationships. As we learn to let God heal our hearts with His love, we can learn new tools that open our hearts to the kinds of relationships we've always wanted.

Openness is half of a key to the greatest relationships of your life. Without openness, we cannot receive good input, wisdom, love, hope, connection, ideas, and everything we need to upgrade our relationships. It is like trying to build a better house with nothing but air. It is tragic how many people we have met who would rather be in an unhealthy relationship and create unhealthy relationships with others because they are not open to changing themselves. We need the right materials to build anything. If we are not open to receiving those materials, everything we try to build will be less than its potential. So, we need to be open to receiving.

This is true relationally. If we are not open to receiving perspectives, ideas, inspiration, impact, and context from others, we will be misguided by assumptions. Of course, we have to examine what we receive, just like we would examine any material we receive. We do not just take it at face value, but we do receive it and examine it and by doing so, receive a lot of great information! Like a child trying new food, we have to learn to withhold judgment until we see the fruit of something.

The second half of your key is based on ownership. Openness, learning, and awareness do no good at all if we do not move into a place of owning, implementing, and stewarding those ideas in our life. One of my (Ally's) greatest breakthroughs in life was when I was a teen. I had been living with a victim mentality, and one day I was so miserable and tired of it, I decided to try to take ownership. Now, I was a victim in some situations; I didn't do anything to deserve to be a victim. No one deserves to be a victim. But, when I decided to take ownership to learn everything I could to make sure that situation never happened again, I became confident, aware, educated, and empowered to feel free to live instead of being fearful of everything and everyone I encountered. It was the most dramatic change that has led me to a place of sustained joy and peace.

If we're going to learn to love, we have to be an owner! To be an owner is to take responsibility for your relationships, choices, thoughts, words, and actions. To gain freedom to enjoy life! It means recognizing that you can't control anyone but yourself, but as you control yourself, you're capable of intentionally creating your environment. Owners aren't the victims of others, nor do they enable others to be victims! They live their lives by their powerful choice to love, and they build, protect, and value healthy relationships with others just as God builds, protects, and values relationships with them.

When we make connection our highest priority, we are already laying the foundation to experience unconditional love in our relationships. When we make this our highest value, we'll learn the tools and skills to achieve it. A relationship with the goal of connection is a safe place for both people to share their feelings and needs, and to meet each other's needs. This is how intimacy is built. As you work through this book, get ready! This is the beginning of a journey into deeper, more connected relationships with God, yourself, and others!

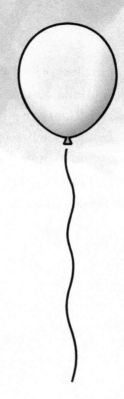

Day 1 – Ownership

OWNING
YOUR LIFE

*"Never be bullied into silence.
Never allow yourself to be made a victim.
Accept no one's definition of your life,
but define yourself."*

Harvey S. Firestone

"Who is wise and understanding among you? Let them show it by their good life, by deeds done in the humility that comes from wisdom."

James 3:13 NIV

What does the word "owner" make you think of? To be an owner is to take responsibility for something. No matter if you own a house, a pet, or a book, you are responsible for paying for it and keeping it clean and in good condition. When we take ownership of our life, we realize we alone let people impact us, or not. We are the ones directing traffic, allowing helpful, life-giving relationships in, and setting boundaries with destructive ones. James 3:13 says, "Who is wise and understanding among you? Let them show it by their good life, by deeds done in the humility that comes from wisdom." Owners are people who shape their lives through their choices and actions, and create environments in which love can grow and thrive.

Life doesn't "happen" to people with a high degree of ownership any more than electricity "happens" to stay on in their house. They don't live on the defense, blaming circumstances and others for how their lives have turned out. Instead, they live on the offense, choosing the life they want to live and taking steps to create that, regardless of how others behave. Owners understand it's not their job to care for or control anyone else's' house, only their own. Instead of trying to get others to be respectful, they create a respectful environment that does not tolerate disrespect. Instead of trying to get others to love them, they remain open to loving others. They set a standard for how they're willing to be treated. The only people they allow to get close to them are people who are also willing to take responsibility for their lives and how they love.

Jesus never let anyone else dictate the values by which He lived. He never blamed Adam or Eve or you for "making" Him have to die on the cross. He also didn't die to try to manipulate you or force you into being saved against your will. He knew it was His choice and He owned it. He gave us the choice to follow, or not. When Jesus encountered the rich young man in Luke 18, the man chose not to give up his riches and follow Jesus. Jesus didn't try to control or shame the other man. He simply said, "This is what's required to come closer to me." We can imitate Him by choosing who we allow to get close to us, and choosing how we protect those connections. We start to become an owner of our life by deciding what we want in life, what kind of relationships we value, and what kind of environments we want to create around us. Then, we get to choose what we're going to do to learn and grow in ways that help us go after it!

Prayer

Thank You, Jesus, that being an owner is already in my DNA!
Thank You that my spirit is naturally attuned to truth,
and Your grace empowers me in new and exciting ways as I align myself with it.
My environment and relationships were made to thrive, and I trust You
to teach me to walk in the fruits of the spirit, especially self-control,
so that I can walk powerfully into the life You have for me!
I choose to live as an owner and to take responsibility for my choices
and actions. You put everything in me to do this!

Reflection

1. Think of someone in your life who models taking ownership. What do they do and say that demonstrates this?

    _____
    _____
    _____
    _____

2. Where in the Bible can you think of Jesus defining His values and making responsible choices?

    _____
    _____
    _____
    _____

3. In which areas of your life do you feel you behave responsibly vs. reckless?

    _____
    _____
    _____
    _____

4. What would change if you accepted more of the ownership God has given you today?

    _____
    _____
    _____
    _____

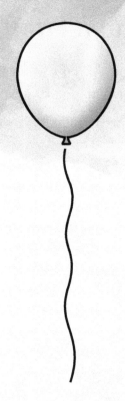

Day 2~ Openness

BEING OPEN TO CHANGING OUR MINDSETS

*"Words cannot only create emotions; they create actions.
And from our actions flow the results of our lives."*

Tony Robbins

"For with God nothing will be impossible."

Luke 1:37 New King James Version

e can live empowered lives, and reach our calling and destiny with confidence in God and ourselves, only if we are open to changing thoughts and mindsets that hold us back. Unhelpful mindsets can delay or even cut off our destiny, love, or connection on a daily basis. If we can become aware of those mindsets that disempower us, we can start to invest in strategies to shift our mindsets to be more in line with God's word, which tells us that "with God nothing will be impossible." This requires an open mind to see what God is doing and thinking, knowing it may not be like anything we imagined. Our word choice often demonstrates if we are open or closed to God doing "a new thing." It may sound like "I can't do that" or "I don't want to hear what you have to say." These words demonstrate we are closed off to even considering what God is saying.

Numbers 13 reminds us of the power of our mindsets and the language that is the fruit produced from those mindsets. God gave the land to the Israelites and spies and went to scout out the promised land. However, we see that the spies responded with different words about it. Caleb said, "We must go up and take possession of the land, for we can certainly conquer it!" But other spies were not open to this idea, even though God was behind it. They responded, "We cannot go up against the people, for they are stronger..." These words of "I can't" led to grumbling, sorrow, despair, anger, frustration, false accusations toward God, and a desire to return to bondage and slavery! Ultimately, these words led them to wander in the wilderness for forty years and miss their destiny. Our mindsets and words are so important!

If we can begin to identify these empowered thoughts through our speech, we can begin to recognize where our thoughts are not aligned with God. We can start to replace them with God's words: "For with God nothing will be impossible." This is a simple but powerful tool. Where our thoughts go, our behavior follows. This means that even if we do not fully believe a thought, our intention to replace unhelpful thoughts will already impact our behavior in small ways, and more so, the more we practice. When God thinks and speaks of you, He does not speak of what you can't do and your limitations. Those thoughts do not enter His mind. He knows that Jesus already provided all the grace that is needed to fill the gaps, and He has full confidence in that grace! Will you accept His grace?

———— ✦ ————

Prayer

God, thank You that with You nothing is impossible.
Thank You for giving me everything I need to grow in self-control,
to manage myself, my thoughts, and to take responsibility for my actions.
As I live in communion with You, I am always empowered to hear Your voice of love!
You have the best thoughts about me and I desire to hear You all my life.
I can do wonderful things in my life because of Your support.
You strengthen me in ways that I can only imagine.
All things are possible with You, Jesus.

Reflection

1. Where do you most often use the words, "I can't" "I have to" or "I'll try"?

   _____

   _____

   _____

   _____

2. What scriptures come to mind about these situations?

   _____

   _____

   _____

   _____

3. What do you think God's thoughts are about these situations?

   _____

   _____

   _____

   _____

4. How can you remind yourself of God's thoughts and/or keep yourself from falling into the trap of using powerless words?

   _____

   _____

   _____

   _____

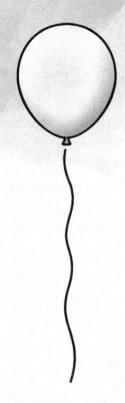

Day 3 – Ownership

TAKING OWNERSHIP OF OUR THOUGHTS

*"Communication is a skill that you can learn.
It's like riding a bicycle or typing. If you're willing to work at it,
you can rapidly improve the quality of every part of your life."*

Brian Tracy

"But the fruit of the Spirit is love, joy, peace, longsuffering, kindness, goodness, faithfulness, gentleness, and self-control. Against such there is no law."

Galatians 5:22-23 NKJV

We set good boundaries around our thoughts when we recognize they are valuable, but not always the full truth. In healthy relationships, both people are responsible for sharing their thoughts, and both people are responsible for valuing the other person's thoughts. Galatians 5:22 tells us that the fruit of the Spirit is "love, joy, peace, longsuffering, kindness, goodness, faithfulness, gentleness and self-control." When we flow freely in these things, we're able to cultivate the mutual respect necessary for healthy relationships.

Here is a situation I often hear about: a wife sees that a co-worker's husband brought that co-worker flowers at work one day. She feels jealous and hurt that her husband has never done that. She starts to think, Maybe he doesn't love me as much as I thought. She wants so badly to feel reassurance she is cared for, but instead of acknowledging her thoughts about the situation and communicating them, she thinks about her anger and perceived rejection. When she sees her husband later, she's furious. He asks her what the matter is, but she responds with, "Like you care!" He's confused. He knows he cares, and feels hurt and disconnected from her because he feels she is withholding and that she doesn't trust him to help. Finally, she yells, "You don't love me! You never bring me flowers." The next day, he brings her flowers, but she isn't pleased because she had to ask for it. He feels powerless and discouraged. "What do you want from me?" he yells, and he throws the flowers on the floor, thinking she is probably enjoying rejecting his efforts. She bursts into tears, convinced his anger is evidence that he doesn't care. They spiral into disconnection.

This example shows why it is important to practice communicating our thoughts, and demonstrate self-control by putting boundaries up with our thoughts and by validating the thoughts communicated by others. When the wife first thinks a fear-based thought about her husband, she can learn to take ownership to recognize the fear and hold the boundaries of respecting her husband's feelings. She might then say, "Hey Honey, I feel afraid right now because someone else got flowers at work today. I had a fear of what would happen if I was not loved as much as I wanted to be. Can you help reassure me?" This is what an owner does. It is a move that increases connection and empowers the husband to help demonstrate care in a way that is more authentic to her, because she is not telling him what to do. When we set boundaries around our relationships that protect mutual respect, both people in the relationship have space to share their thoughts. When we set boundaries around our feelings and communicate around our feelings, it opens the door for our relationships to be all that we long for them to be!

Prayer

God, thank You that You designed relationships to increase in depth as we get to know people better. I choose not to "camp out" in the safe, surface-level of relationships, but to build heart-to-heart connections with others by communicating honestly my thoughts and needs, and valuing the thoughts of others. I want to listen to Your voice all the time. Your words bring the fruit of the spirit and bring in so many good things. I desire to set my affections on you and set up my actions and boundaries around Your thoughts and not just my own. Your thoughts are higher than mine. Your ways are better than mine. I want to partner with You.

Reflection

1. What are your initial thoughts and reactions to the story shared in this entry?

   _____

   _____

   _____

   _____

2. Can you remember a time when you blindly accepted your feelings, and later found out they did not tell the whole story? What happened? How did it impact your relationships?

   _____

   _____

   _____

   _____

3. How might it impact your relationships if you were able to value the commitment to connection more than commitment to your feelings?

   _____

   _____

   _____

   _____

4. What are the benefits to sharing your feelings and needs in a relationship? What are the risks?

   _____

   _____

   _____

   _____

Day 4 ~ Openness

PRODUCTIVE VS. UNPRODUCTIVE DISAGREEMENTS

"Our maturity will be judged by how well we are able to agree to disagree and yet continue to love one another, to care for one another, and cherish one another and seek the greater good of the other."

Desmond Tutu

"And yet I show you a more excellent way."

1 Corinthians 12:31 NKJV

ny two people can disagree and argue, but if there is no openness to resolution, these "talks" become activities that go nowhere and make the relationship worse! Talking is only communicating when it has a goal and a purpose. Jeremy had a friendship where disagreements came up, and it felt like the conversations were going around in never-ending circles. Problems were discussed, but despite his desire to resolve things, no ownership was taken by the other party to resolve them.

Discussing problems and even needs without a goal to resolve them only sows frustration and disconnection. If there is not a shared goal to resolve issues, a disagreement becomes a fight about who is good, bad, right, or wrong. Disagreements become a vehicle for wounding words, blame, and anger instead of an opportunity to be known, understood, heard, respected, and to build deeper connection and commitment to being on the same team. Working toward a resolution can be hard, because it requires us to let go of all-or-nothing thinking and think more complexly about possible solutions. But this conversation places both parties as teammates, increasing their bond as they overcome obstacles and disagreements together.

In his letter to Timothy, Paul warns against getting involved in pointless arguments that serve nobody. Instead, he tells us to pursue righteousness, faith, love, and peace. 1 Corinthians 12:31 tells us that there may be many ways to do something, but God has a "most excellent way." When we look for the most excellent way for relationships, we realize our communication goals should be to demonstrate our value for others and ourselves, and be open to learn from each other's thoughts, feelings, or needs, so we can be good teammates to them. When we set our goals with this in mind, we're able to have fruitful, positive disagreements.

<hr>

Prayer

*God, thank You for valuing connection above all else.
Where I'm clinging to the need to be right or for someone else to acknowledge they are wrong, I release this to You now. Thank You for the grace to choose connection, just like You do. Thank You for the freedom I can walk in when I look for solutions instead of problems! You see the road ahead of me and deeply desire to show me this road. Thank You, God, for giving me vision and goals for the future.
I can bring these into every relationship and communication.
I desire to move forward in my communication with You
and with others with very clear goals in mind.
Thank You for helping me with this.*

Reflection

1. Where have you experienced "relationship killers" in conversations?

    _____
    _____
    _____
    _____

2. How has it impacted your relationships when you feel heard and valued versus unheard and unvalued?

    _____
    _____
    _____
    _____

3. What new goals would you like to set for future conversations?

    _____
    _____
    _____
    _____

4. Which relationships in your life would benefit from setting the goals to listen, value, and learn?

    _____
    _____
    _____
    _____

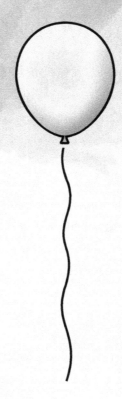

Day 5– Ownership

TAKING OWNERSHIP
OF OUR EMOTIONS

"Emotions can get in the way or get you on the way."

Mavis Mazhura

"Keep your heart with all diligence,
For out of it spring the issues of life."

Proverbs 4:23 NKJV

etting boundaries around our emotions can be one of the most important things we do. You've probably heard people talk about emotional intelligence, and how important it is to be successful in all kinds of relationships. It sounds like something would take time to learn, but actually emotional intelligence is about one thing: taking responsibility for our emotions. Proverbs 4:23 says, "Keep your heart with all diligence, For out of it spring the issues of life." We take responsibility for our emotions by taking time to understand the message they are sending us, and learning skills to manage them.

Our emotions do not tell the truth, but they tell us the truth of our experience, which could be objectively right or very wrong. Uncomfortable emotions show up to tell us that either we need to change, our situation needs to change, or our thoughts need to change. If we do not get the message, we will not know what to do to resolve the message, and we will stay stuck in fear. If we take time to receive messages, process them, and resolve them, we are finally taking ownership of them. If we are in conversations with someone who is constantly unable to resolve their emotions toward us or the relationship, that is a sign they are not taking ownership. If we see someone constantly blaming others for their feelings, they are missing the message the feeling is sending altogether. Feelings are there for YOU and no one can make you feel anything unless you decide to accept that feeling as well. No one can "make" you feel loved unless you accept it from them, and no one can "make" you feel angry unless you accept it as well. Your partnership is what makes the feeling yours, or not.

In Luke 9, Jesus is on His way to Jerusalem and needs somewhere to stay for the night. A certain village doesn't welcome Him. James and John are horrified. They have a strong emotional reaction and ask Jesus if He wants them to call down fire and burn up the whole village! Jesus reminds them of truth in the midst of their emotions, no doubt reminding them that He came to give life, not end it. If we make decisions from emotions and do not have boundaries with them, we will react in ways that are destructive toward others, and to us! Instead, if we can set boundaries around how much of a voice our emotions have, we will make decisions that bring life to us and our relationships.

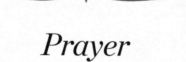

Prayer

*What a gift to have emotions that let me know what's going on inside me.
Thank You for giving me the ability to receive messages in the form of
uncomfortable emotions, so that I can pause and understand what I need to change
to be emotionally healthy. I accept the responsibility that comes with this gift,
knowing that You, God, never give me more than I am capable of managing.
You empower me to rule over the earth and over myself. Today, I choose
to rule my emotions with patience, kindness, and understanding.
Jesus, reign supreme over all my emotions!*

Reflection

1.   How good are you at giving a voice to your emotions; are some easier to voice than others?

     _____

     _____

     _____

     _____

2.   Do you feel you have a process in place to listen as your emotions come up, or do you tend to stuff them all in and then feel like they explode everywhere later?

     _____

     _____

     _____

     _____

3.   How might you start to make room for accepting the emotions you have and empower yourself to address them one at a time?

     _____

     _____

     _____

     _____

4.   How might you set a boundary with your emotions today and make a decision to allow your emotions to bring life to you?

     _____

     _____

     _____

     _____

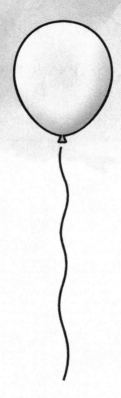

Day 6 – Openness

OPEN MINDSETS VS.
CLOSED MINDSETS

"Faith, as Paul saw it, was a living, flaming thing leading to surrender and obedience to the commandments of Christ."

A.W. Tozer

"The world and its desires pass away,
but whoever does the will of God lives forever"

1 John 2:17 NIV

magine you are planning a good surprise for someone, but when you ask them to come share in it, they respond, "I won't!" What would you think or feel next? I think this is how God feels at times when He asks us to do something. To me, whenever I hear "I won't," it feels inflexible, stuck, stubborn, unreachable, and closed. Have you ever been on the other end of "I won't?" If you have, you'll know it's a quick connection killer, and often feels like an attempt by one person to exert power over another. As we learn to recognize this powerless language, we can find tools and strategies to turn these situations around and move toward openness and connection.

When God asked Jonah to go to Nineveh, he responded with a clear and stubborn, "I won't." He was not open to discussion; he didn't want to go, and his reaction was to run away. Even when the storm rose, Jonah didn't open up conversation with God, but let himself be thrown overboard. I wonder what he was so afraid of that death seemed like a better option than being obedient to God? Fear of being wrong? Fear of not getting his way? Idolatry of his own views and thoughts? One thing's for sure, he shut down the connection between him and God. It was only when Jonah was in the fish's belly that the scripture tells us, "In my distress I called to God, and He answered me." When his heart softened and the stubbornness of "I won't" turned to openness and willingness to talk about it, everything changed. 1 John 2:17 says, "The world and its desires pass away, but whoever does the will of God lives forever." Your desires and thoughts, if not from God, will lead to nothing. God's goal in directing us is to show His love to us by leading us into abundant, eternal life. When we say, "I won't," to God, it cuts off our access to an abundant life.

In our other relationships, "I won't" is a powerless mindset because it reveals fear, a lack of trust, and seeks to control through inflexibility. "I won't" is effectively a barrier that one person puts up in a relationship. It says, "You can come no further. I'm not open to brainstorming other solutions; I don't want to talk about better solutions; I do not want compromise; I do not want you and your thoughts, voice, or ideas involved in our relationship." Essentially saying, "I do not want you to be here at all. I only want me." Saying, "I won't," is an attempt to exert control. It may feel powerful, but it shuts down connection and solutions. We overcome this mindset when we confront the fear that keeps us from allowing others to be present and impact us, and to open up the lines of communication again. When we let go of fear, control, and idolatry in our own way, we keep connections open. We live from a mindset that keeps us moving forward in our relationships.

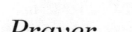

Prayer

*God, thank You for giving me the freedom to see what is possible,
when I am open to seeing from Your perspective. I choose today
to make choices to remain open to learning and growing, to not allow fear
to get a foothold in my life and relationships. You break the bondage
of fear that keeps me from jumping into new opportunities and love.
I will pursue You and the life You give me without hesitation and fear.
I will love like You loved me. You are wonderful, Jesus.
Thank You for showing me Your "can do" spirit.
You are my love.*

Reflection

1. When, where, or with whom have you felt "I won't" rise up in you?

    _____

    _____

    _____

    _____

2. What are the fears that trigger an "I won't" response in you, and what is God's truth about them?

    _____

    _____

    _____

    _____

3. Have you ever experienced a break in connection as a result of inflexibility on someone's part?

    _____

    _____

    _____

    _____

4. In which of your relationships do you feel it's most important to remove your fear or stubbornness and increase your openness?

    _____

    _____

    _____

    _____

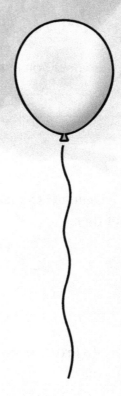

Day 7 – Ownership

OWNERSHIP IN RELATIONSHIPS

"When you have too many top priorities, you effectively have no top priorities."

Stephen Covey

"When the Day of Pentecost had fully come, they were all with one accord in one place."

Acts 2:1 NKJV

People who take ownership for their relationships are the type of people others want to be with. They protect their relationships according to their priorities, and set appropriate boundaries in line with these priorities. Consumers, or people who do not take ownership, approach relationships from a place of desperation. Relationships are hard and never feel like enough because they and those they would be in a relationship with do not know their priorities. We've all experienced people like this, who want more than we're able to give over and over again.

It is our job, as people who take ownership, to manage consumers by saying a simple "no." It is their job to manage their reaction to our no. None of us can do that for them. It is also your job to manage your reaction to the "no" others give you. It's your responsibility to assess what limits are necessary to protect connection, and grow and maintain healthy relationships. Healthy relationships happen when two people choose each other and take full ownership for that choice. That choice is ownership of each moment and decision individually, and then walking it out together. In every relationship, other people will come and look for our attention, help, or affection. We get to set limits on what these people have access to based on our priorities.

Ally had already taken full ownership of the direction of her life, emotional health, happiness, and success in life before meeting Jeremy.

She knew because of that, she did not need a man to add something that was missing, and was not going to settle for anyone who did not add to what she had built. She was protective of it, putting up boundaries around her time to the point that she only offered Jeremy one hour of her time on their first date! Once she saw more of who Jeremy was, and that their values matched, she offered more time and energy accordingly. Jeremy came with the same high ownership and value for what he brought to the table, and was not going to settle for someone who did not equally value those things, which Ally did. Our ownership level matched, and that created a mutual trust, commitment, and value that makes our relationship very easy. Ally often says that she still has never "fallen" in love; she deliberately "stepped" into love with Jeremy because she saw the fruit of it was good, consistent, healthy, and growing. People who take ownership do not fall in or out of love based on what others do; they make it a conscious decision. They choose what they will do (in this case, love) and choose what they will not do (offer time to things that do not align with their values).

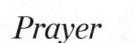

Prayer

God, thank You that Your Spirit is the spirit of unity.
Thank You, Jesus, that the Father, Son, and Holy Spirit are one,
and You desire me to be one with You and other people.
I stand firmly on the trust that Your desire is for me to have healthy relationships.
Where relationships are broken, I thank You that You are the God of restoration.
Build with me a beautiful home for my relationships.
Show me how to lead in my relationships with health in mind.
I want to protect like you projected those the Father gave you.
Show me Your ways, my friend Jesus.

Reflection

1. Do you feel fully empowered to choose who you spend time with, or do you often feel manipulated or pressured into things?

   _____

   _____

   _____

   _____

2. What might be a kind phrase you can use to put up a boundary and say no the next time you feel pressured into something?

   _____

   _____

   _____

   _____

3. Do you have some relationships where others seem to have less ownership than you? Write about why this may be, and what steps God might have you take in these relationships.

   _____

   _____

   _____

   _____

4. What are some things you do or might do to protect your healthy relationships?

   _____

   _____

   _____

   _____

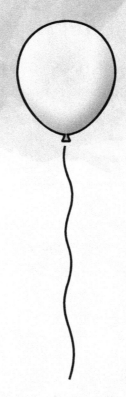

Day 8– Openness

SHOWING APPRECIATION

"Wherever there is appreciation, there is duplication."

T. D. Jakes

"Finally, brethren, whatever things are true, whatever things are noble, whatever things are just, whatever things are pure, whatever things are lovely, whatever things are of good report, if there is any virtue and if there is anything praiseworthy — meditate on these things."

Philippians 4:8 NKJV

We pave the way for increased intimacy with God through appreciation. If we are too closed off, or focused on ourselves and our problems, we cannot truly enter His gates! Psalm 100 tells us that we "enter into his gates with thanksgiving." A thankful heart is an open heart. This is the key to entering into God's presence, expressing our love to Him and receiving His love for us. It also unlocks joy in us as we are open to acknowledging what we've been given, and it releases hope and expectation for what the future may hold. We see appreciation is a core type of communication Jesus has with Father God. In John 11:41, He thanks the Father for hearing Him. In John 6:11, He thanks God before doing a miracle. In Luke 22:17 and 19, He thanks God before the first communion. If we are made in the image of God, and meant to model our lives after Jesus, it is important we learn to communicate appreciation.

Experts say that to have a good relationship, we should be open to sharing a bare minimum of five positive thoughts about the relationship or person to every one request for change or negative thought. Learning to communicate our appreciation tends to improve our communication with others. Voicing our appreciation for others opens up a safe space where trust can grow. Like Jesus with the loaves and fishes, as we give thanks for what is there (instead of frustration at what is not), we make room for the good to multiply. When appreciation is communicated to us it tends to lower the fear that we might be judged, controlled, or criticized. We feel seen in the relationship. We're more likely to offer free gifts of affection and look for ways to share "I love you" messages that create safety and deepen connection.

One way to improve any conversation is to start off with appreciation. This ensures our heart is right and enables the other person to be more receptive to other things we have to say. We see this often practiced in many of Paul's letters. In 1 Corinthians 1, Paul does not open his letter with rebuke, but instead, he says in verse 4, "I thank my God always concerning you for the grace of God which was given to you by Christ Jesus." In Philippians 4:8, Paul also reminds us "...if there is any virtue and if there is anything praiseworthy—meditate on these things." When you build a habit of expressing gratitude and appreciation out loud, it creates fertile soil for your relationship and communication to be enriched. In the same way, when we express our gratitude to God for the many blessings in our lives, we pave the way for a deeper connection with Him.

———————— ✦ ————————

Prayer

God, I am excited to go on an adventure of discovering just how much I can appreciate in You and those around me. Thank You that as I begin to appreciate what I have, it begins to multiply and my heart begins to be more aligned with yours. I want to take time today to recognize and thank You for the people You have put in my life. Thank You to those who have brought strength, joy, and even growth to my life. I choose to appreciate them today, not just in my thoughts but in words. I commit to being somebody who speaks out my appreciation for others.

Reflection

1. Write down two things you are thankful you can see, two things you are thankful you can smell, two things you are thankful you can hear, two things you are thankful you can touch, and two things you are thankful you can taste. What difference do you notice in your mind and mood as you become aware of gratitude?

    _____
    _____
    _____
    _____

2. What difference in thoughts and mood do you experience when others demonstrate awareness of what you have to offer instead of focusing on what you lack? How does it impact your connection?

    _____
    _____
    _____
    _____

3. Who is someone you think does not often experience others gratitude?

    _____
    _____
    _____
    _____

4. What good might you be able to call out to that person today?

    _____
    _____
    _____
    _____

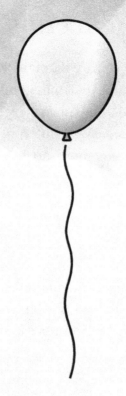

Day 9 – Openness

CULTIVATING
REAL HAPPINESS

*"The happiest people don't have the best of everything;
they just make the best of everything!"*

Dr. Caroline Leaf

"The precepts of the Lord are right, giving joy to the heart. The commands of the Lord are radiant, giving light to the eyes."

Psalm 19:8 NIV

When we follow Jesus and step into the fulfillment He offers, we often have to let go of old patterns and behaviors. When we embrace our wholeness journey with Jesus, we realize that our happiness is our responsibility alone, and make choices to prioritize cultivating this for ourselves. It is unhelpful to approach relationships as consumers, looking for what the relationship will give us. Looking for people who have resources of love, happiness, comfort, and joy to offer because we don't have it ourselves. The thing is, someone else's happiness will never fill us up, or cause us to be happy. In fact, we may even become resentful of that person for not meeting this need. As Jeremy would say, you don't win a football game by watching the good plays everyone else makes. You win by focusing on creating and executing your best plays. We find our own source of happiness when we embrace a life of ownership and wholeness with God at the center.

You are a responsible person with the capacity to make decisions, including decisions about your emotions! It's important to understand this, because otherwise we go looking in all the wrong places to find happiness, most commonly in other people. We may look at somebody else's resources of love, happiness, comfort, and joy and decide they must be the answer to our happiness as well! The Psalms tell us that our source of joy is God within us. "The precepts of the Lord are right, giving joy to the heart. The commands of the Lord are radiant, giving light to the eyes!" (Psalm 19:18). As responsible people, we know how to access

50

joy and happiness and become a resource for others, rather than look to them for what is our responsibility to cultivate.

In Mark 10, a rich young ruler comes to Jesus and asks what it would take to get eternal life. Jesus tells him to follow the commandments in the scriptures. The ruler confirms that he has always done so. So, Jesus asks him to take another step and sell everything he owns to follow Him. The rich young ruler walks away, sadly, unwilling to give up earthly riches for a life with Jesus. There was a cost to the fulfillment the rich young ruler was asking for. He recognized that Jesus could offer him something of worth, but he wanted it without having to let anything go. Part of following God is allowing Him to be our joy, and letting go of trying to get joy in things that are not helpful and do not produce life! He has put within each of us keys that unlock our unique access to our own happiness and fulfillment. What does it cost us? It costs us our willingness to give up what we might value and feel we need the most: our negative and disempowering thoughts and emotions. We must surrender this at the feet of Jesus, and embrace the happiness He and His Word give.

Prayer

God, I fully embrace my wholeness journey with You!
I know that you lead me into all joy, that You teach me how to be an owner and to let others around me be owners as well. Thank You that as I embrace Your truth, old patterns and behaviors fall off me, and I can discover Your ways of doing this. Where I've looked outside of myself for happiness, I now rejoice in the fact that I can cultivate this within myself, and my expectation is that it will bubble over and become a resource for others. I take full responsibility for my life today with your help, and look to the bright future You have for me.

Reflection

1.   Identify some things in life that make you happy.

_____

_____

_____

_____

2.   How can you integrate more of these things, or aspects of these things, into your daily life in big or small ways?

_____

_____

_____

_____

3.   What is an area of life where you have historically struggled to be happy or have joy?

_____

_____

_____

_____

4.   What choice can you make to cultivate more happiness in this area?

_____

_____

_____

_____

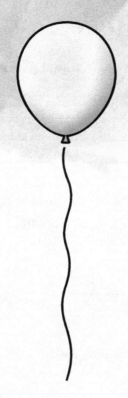

Day 10 – Ownership

TAKING OWNERSHIP OF YOUR PROBLEMS

"All problems become smaller when you confront them instead of dodging them."

William F. Halsey

"But let each one test his own work, and then his reason to boast will be in himself alone and not in his neighbor. For each will have to bear his own load"

If we're not taking ownership of our problems, we're either hoping somebody else will fix them or expecting a magical solution to take them away. Neither of these are good options! No one would have this strategy for their home or car, so why do people take this strategy with their life and relationships? At the end of the day, some people will choose to let their house fall into disrepair, but they cannot expect you to give up your life to repair it for them. You can help them repair it out of the abundance of time, resources, and energy you have, but you should never feel like it is your problem to solve.

When people fall into control, they do just that; they try to choose the furniture, design, and paint color of the home everyone else lives in each day. None of us would stand for that! But, many of us allow people to manipulate us emotionally to change or give up ownership of our decisions and our agency to create change. We listen too much when they say we should be more of this or less of that. We take their word as more valid than God's word, and we trust people to make decisions they have no long-term ownership of.

As we take ownership of our own problems, we also have to practice allowing others to own their problems, too. Have you ever felt like you're investing more time in somebody else's problem than they are? It's okay to ask for help with our problems, but until we take ownership for them and let others do the same with theirs, we won't find long-term solutions and see them solved. It is important to ask ourselves and others, "What can I do now to start to solve this problem?" If you are unsure, get expert advice, but don't sit around waiting when God has given you stewardship of your life. Galatians 6:4-5 says, "But let each one test his own work, and then his reason to boast will be in himself alone and not in his neighbor. For each will have to bear his own load." This verse tells us that while others can offer us their resources to help us, we must take responsibility for what is ours and allow others to take responsibility for what is theirs.

Prayer

God, thank You for saying I'm more than a conqueror!
Where I've blamed others or waited for others to make decisions for me,
I now take ownership. I count myself fortunate to no longer be stuck, not knowing
that I have the power of Christ that raised Jesus from the dead in me!
I know because of Your promises, I already have everything I need
to overcome any situation or problem I am facing without shame or guilt.
You are faithful to lead me into victory in every area of my life.

Reflection

1. Are there problems in your life that you are hoping or expecting others to solve?

   _____

   _____

   _____

   _____

2. Are there problems that belong to other people that you are currently trying to solve instead of supporting them in solving their own problem?

   _____

   _____

   _____

   _____

3. How might you help them to establish them as the wonder of their problem and solution?

   _____

   _____

   _____

   _____

4. Are there things, situations, dreams, or relationships you have given up on that God might want you to continue to try to find solutions for?

   _____

   _____

   _____

   _____

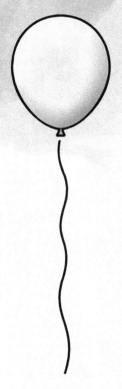

Day 11 – Ownership

PROTECTING
RELATIONSHIPS

"It's more important to be kind than to be right."

Bianca Olthoff

"And above all things have fervent love for one another, for love will cover a multitude of sins"

1 Peter 4:8 NKJV

The story of scripture is the story of God doing everything possible to restore and protect His relationship with His people. This is because unconditional love is His nature, and He wanted to make sure that nothing will ever get between Him and His people. No matter what we do, God has made sure that our relationship with Him is always protected. 1 Peter 4:8 says, "And above all things have fervent love for one another, for love will cover a multitude of sins." This verse invites us to extend the unconditional love we have from the Father to others. Fervent love pushes past offenses, disappointments, and bad behavior and chooses to protect connection no matter what!

Protecting connection is about extending unconditional love. It says, "No matter what you share with me, or how I feel about it, my love for you isn't at stake here. I will keep moving toward you no matter what." It's when we establish this that real, honest, and healing conversations can happen, conversations that lead to a deeper, more intimate connection. Establishing this in your relationships looks like communicating and trusting each other to do what it takes to protect the connection. It means learning to talk to each other about our thoughts, feelings, and needs in the relationship rather than hiding them and feeling resentful. As we adjust to each other's feedback and meet each other's needs, we build trust and strengthen our relationship.

Jesus shows this throughout scripture. A great example of Jesus protecting connection is when He reappears to His disciples after His resurrection. Thomas doubted Him, and Peter denied Him three times, but in both cases, Jesus never took away His unconditional love for them even though there was clear conflict. He meets Thomas in his doubt and gives him an answer. He meets Peter in his shame, and commissions him into his purpose.

In fact, no matter what His disciples do, Jesus never turns His love off toward them. Jesus protects the connection above right or wrong, good or bad behavior. Can you imagine living this way? A practical step toward this is to learn to take a break and connect when things get heated. You can acknowledge the unresolved issue, but eat a meal together, go for a walk, or find another way to connect before continuing the conversation. By doing this, you're protecting the connection. You are telling each other, "You are what's most important, not your behavior." If we can learn to value connection over being right, winning arguments, or getting our point across, we enter the holy grail of relationships—unconditional love and acceptance.

Prayer

God, thank You for choosing me. Thank You that Your priority is always to protect your connection with me. You're more interested in a relationship with me than whether what I'm doing is right or wrong. You have my heart, Jesus. Bring forth the abundance of Your love and connection in our relationship. I choose to protect connection in my close relationships in this way, too. Guide me to see connection as the main priority in every one of my relationships. With my every action, every word, let my life build a beautiful home for people to dwell in harmony

Reflection

1. In your relationship with God, are you currently experiencing any feelings of disconnection?

    _____

    _____

    _____

    _____

2. Consider how this might show you your fears of rejection, mistakes, or judgment.

    _____

    _____

    _____

    _____

3. How can you extend the Grace of God and choose connection with others instead of judging, shaming, or using unhealthy anger toward others? Toward a specific person?

    _____

    _____

    _____

    _____

4. How can you pursue connection to help others to experience confidence and peace in your relationship with them?

    _____

    _____

    _____

    _____

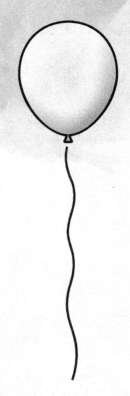

Day 12– Openness

LEARNING
HOW TO LOVE

"God created you to be a gift of His love to others."

Jack Frost

> *"But if you love those who love you, what credit is that to you? For even sinners love those who love them…but love your enemies, do good to them, and lend to them, expecting nothing in return."*

Most people have an unconscious attitude of "I will only love you if you're just like me." We find it easy to love people who are like us because we can more easily relate to them and do not feel challenged by them. But real love is bigger than this. Luke 6:32 is an invitation to learn to love more deeply, and to love through our differences. Jesus was our perfect model. He crossed all kinds of barriers, hung out with people vastly different from Himself, and accepted them no matter what. He knew that He didn't need to control anyone but Himself. He knew He was already abundantly and unconditionally loved by God, so He did not fear differences, even ones that led Him to be rejected by people. He wasn't afraid to pour love out unconditionally on people who were different from Him. In fact, He embraced the differences!

We, Jeremy and Ally, have had people who have watched us work and travel together try to explain away why we don't argue by saying, "It is probably so easy for you to get along so well because you are exactly alike!" These people had no idea. In fact, we have different (and strong) views on politics, social issues, education, spending, saving, investing, cars (classic car vs. a Prius), entertainment, style, being vegetarian, and so much more. We have different personalities, strengths, and communication styles. Now, it is true we both love God, working hard, and helping people, and we also have some superficial similar interests. But way more important than that, we are the same in this certain way:

62

we both place a very high value on openness and ownership for how we show up in our relationship. We value respecting others more than trying to control their opinion. We resolve disagreements with grace, faith, respect and love, instead of escalating disagreements with attempts to control through arguing and fighting.

True love is about our ability to accept and even appreciate differences. When you have surrendered your "right" to control the activity, meal, movie, budget, conversation, or political views of the other, your relationship becomes full of life and enriching. We're able to move into a whole new level of a relationship—one that embraces the richness that difference brings instead of being fearful of it, and one that lets everybody be themselves, even when that means they're harder for us to understand. Learning to love looks like going from control to self-control, from fear to love, and choosing love in the midst of our differences! If we can do this, we'll see a whole new level of love released in our lives.

Prayer

*God, love is Your highest priority and it is Your desire for Your children
to learn to love well. Thank you that love comes in lots of different shapes and sizes,
and is an overflow of each person's heart. Thank You that as I commit to learning
how to love as you love, You increase my capacity for more! Teach me
the nuances of Your heart and process. I want to listen to Your heart
just like John the Beloved did when he lay on Your chest.
You alone, Lord, are the embodiment of love for the world to see.
Teach me, show me, and love me.*

Reflection

1. Identify several people who are not like you, and whom you may find hard to love (you don't have to write down their names). Would you want to be around them more if they thought, spoke, or acted more like you?

   _____

   _____

   _____

   _____

2. Shift the focus from what they need to change, to what you can change to love them as they are.

   _____

   _____

   _____

   _____

3. Forgive yourself for your judgment. Forgive them for not being like you, thinking like you, acting like you.

   _____

   _____

   _____

   _____

4. Seek to identify and thank God for a strength their differences might provide.

   _____

   _____

   _____

   _____

Day 13 – Ownership

BUILDING
RELATIONSHIPS

"The human heart will seek to be known, understood, and connected with above all else. If you do not connect, the ones you care about will find someone who will."

Dr Henry Cloud

*"And over all these virtues put on love,
which binds them all together in perfect unity"*

Colossians 3:14 NIV

o you ever look at others, wishing you could have the kinds of relationships they have? It's great to have relationship role models, but as God's children, we cannot fall into the trap of thinking those people just "got lucky." With the right tools, great relationships are available to all of us! As we lay good foundations of love in our lives, and reinforce them brick by brick with positive habits, we can all build the relationships we want most.

Just like a house, we must build a relational connection on strong foundations. Colossians 3 tells us to clothe ourselves in compassion, kindness, humility, gentleness, and patience, to forgive each other and to put on love above all the other virtues, because it's love that binds them all together. When we're building connection, these are the bricks that matter. This doesn't mean we need to be perfect at it. It does mean we should actively choose how we build connections, and seek to make small improvements when we can.

These virtues create an atmosphere of love and acceptance. They create an atmosphere where everyone is free to be themselves and communicate their feelings and needs. Each time we communicate and meet each other's needs, another solid brick is put in place for building connection. This means to both offer a safe space for others to communicate their feelings and to communicate honestly ourselves. Every time we do this, we're building and strengthening our relationships.

66

There are few moments so heartbreakingly honest in scripture as Mary Bethany's response to Jesus after her brother Lazarus has died. She is consumed with grief and angry with Jesus, but she does not hide her emotions and needs from Him. Weeping, she says, "Lord, if you had been here, my brother would not have died." Jesus, impacted by her pain, weeps too. He is not weeping for Lazarus, whom He will soon raise. He is weeping for Mary, His friend, who honestly shared her heart with Him. We build connections in moments like these. Next time emotions come up for you, take a step toward connection and share your heart with someone. Practice allowing yourself to be seen.

─────────── ✦ ───────────

Prayer

God, thank You for always leading me to increase.
Thank You for giving me resources, tools, and skills to build connections with others.
Thank You for cheering me on as I grow in forming healthy, lasting relationships,
and demonstrating what it means to love without restraint. I want to build
my connections with You and build my connections with others. You are my guide.
Thank You for showing me what connection is in its purest form.
I love You, Jesus.

Reflection

1. Who is a safe person with whom you feel you can express your true thoughts and needs?

   _____

   _____

   _____

   _____

2. What do you think often gets in the way of honestly sharing how you feel?

   _____

   _____

   _____

   _____

3. Who can you ask for advice about how to better share your thoughts and needs?

   _____

   _____

   _____

   _____

4. How can you better respond with empathy, kindness, compassion, humility, gentleness, patience, and forgiveness when others share their feelings with you? Any of those qualities in particular you may need to work on?

   _____

   _____

   _____

   _____

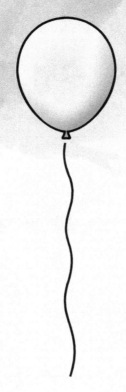

Day 14~ Openness

CHOOSING LOVE
OVER HIDING

"I learned that courage was not the absence of fear,
but the triumph over it. The brave man is not he who does not
feel afraid, but he who conquers that fear."

Nelson Mandela

"There is no fear in love;
but perfect love casts out fear..."

1 John 4:18 NKJV

Fear can do strange things to our minds. Sometimes, especially if a confrontation is unexpected, our thoughts can become jumbled, because we're too scared to say anything. We clam up, freeze, and say nothing while another person desperately tries to get us to understand their point. Freezing, like taking flight, is a fear-based reaction that is most often instinctive. Identifying that this is a normal reaction for us means we can put strategies in place to respond differently when under pressure. When we do this, we protect our relationship from the fear bombs that drive our self-protective instincts.

1 John 4:18 says perfect love casts out all fear! Because of God's love for us, fear-based reactions are no longer our inheritance, and we can learn new ways to respond to confrontation. When we're closed up like a clam, we're not being open, honest, or genuine about how we think or feel. We are not helping or contributing to the relationship. In fact, we're often just hoping that if we stay still long enough, the conversation will blow over or the other person will go away. If our highest value is getting to the other side of the confrontation, we are far more likely to say what we think the person wants to hear rather than what's on our hearts. This does not serve the goal of a strong relationship. While you may temporarily appease the other person, you have created distance between your heart and theirs, which does the relationship no good at all.

If you're a "freezer," learning to communicate how you're feeling is a crucial step in staying connected to the other person during confrontation. When you stop communicating, you will end up stuck with resentments, anger, and the feeling of being unheard. If we can resist the urge to "people please" and see the conversation through to its resolution, we are far more likely to leave the conversation having built trust, confidence, and feeling connected.

Prayer

God, I love to think about how You've watched me grow up from my first day on earth, and will stay by my side all the days of my life. I live in the shadow of Your wings, nestled into Your heart. I know that I don't need to hide, because You've made me in Your image, perfect and complete. Where I've been afraid to show myself, I now find confidence in Your extravagant love for me. Where I've held back in the past, I now get ready to advance because You're with me! Thank You that You've watched me grow up and are aware of every fear I carry in my heart. Thank You for Your perfect plan for me to replace every fear with perfect love, starting today. Where my unconscious response has been to freeze, I now choose to advance!

Reflection

1. Is "clamming up" or freezing a natural reaction for you when you're afraid?

   _____

   _____

   _____

   _____

2. Where have you seen others react to fear in this way?

   _____

   _____

   _____

   _____

3. What do you need to help you overcome fear in these situations?

   _____

   _____

   _____

   _____

4. What could you do to help others feel safe to open up instead of freeze?

   _____

   _____

   _____

   _____

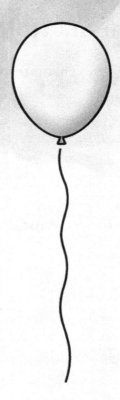

Day 15 – Ownership

WHERE YOUR MIND GOES, YOUR RELATIONSHIP FOLLOWS

"Progress is impossible without change; and those who cannot change their minds cannot change anything."

George Bernard Shaw

"...But we have the mind of Christ."

1 Corinthians 2:16 NKJV

Where do our mindsets come from? We inherit many of our mindsets from our families or other influences. We take them for granted, but this doesn't mean they are correct mindsets, or that they cannot change. If we've inherited mindsets that are helpful for relationships, we can look forward to meaningful and fulfilling connections and relationships. If we have inherited unhelpful mindsets, such as suspicion, fear, anger, and judgment, we can learn to switch them to new, healthy mindsets that protect and nurture our relationships.

1 Corinthians 2:16 tells us that "we have the mind of Christ." Isn't this amazing news? God has already made provision for any unhealthy mindsets by giving us the perfect mind of His son! He knew we wouldn't all inherit perfect mindsets in every area. He also gave us everything we needed to access the mindsets we need to improve our relationships. When we choose to go after a new way of thinking, He is faithful to reveal who He is to us and how He thinks about things.

Once we can learn to identify unhelpful mindsets, we're already halfway to establishing new, powerful patterns in our relationships. In many marriages, friendships, dating relationships, or mentorships, we can shift the responsibility for the quality of our relationship to the other person. "He's not showing me his emotions," or, "She gets aggressive when she's angry and there's no talking to her" are examples of this. The problem is, if we're blaming others for the strength of our relationship, we're partnering with a powerless, unhelpful mindset and are likely to stay stuck.

When we focus on mindsets that are helpful to a relationship, we shift out of blame and recognize we are equally responsible for taking ownership of our relational goal. Helpful mindsets produce the fruit of healthy relationships. In order to truly change our mindsets, we need to exchange the habits and skills we've learned that lead to relational disconnection and humbly work to replace them with habits and skills that will help us reach connection. Does it feel good or easy? No! But most valuable things are not easy to come by. It is the same for all of us; we can all develop new mindsets that serve our true desire for deep, lasting relationships.

Prayer

God, thank You for giving me access to Your mind.
Thank You that as I renew my mind, wrong mindsets fall away and
are replaced by new mindsets grounded in Your truth. I love Your thoughts.
They bring about the abundance of Heaven and the best ways to live our lives.
We have access to this deep well in You and we will turn to You in our mind and
cultivate Your thoughts and dreams for us. Share Your practical, resourceful,
and supernatural thoughts with us, Jesus!

Reflection

1. Which other Bible verses do you know that speak about the power of your mindset?

   _____

   _____

   _____

   _____

2. Where in the past has the Holy Spirit upgraded your mindset? What was the result?

   _____

   _____

   _____

   _____

3. Which area of your life would you most like to receive an `upgraded mindset?

   _____

   _____

   _____

   _____

4. Do you know anyone who models that mindset?

   _____

   _____

   _____

   _____

Day 16 – Openness

RESPONDING
WITH EMPATHY

*"Empathetic listening is an awesome medication
for the hurting heart."*

Gary Chapman

*"Rejoice with those who rejoice, and weep
with those who weep."*

Romans 12:15 NKJV

Relationships provide ample opportunity for dealing with challenging emotions. When we find ourselves in difficult conversations, it's not always easy to discipline ourselves to respond, rather than react, and keep pursuing connection and understanding. One way to train our minds is to intentionally practice empathy—to put ourselves in the other person's shoes and genuinely seek to understand their perspective. Positioning ourselves in this way sets us up to draw close to each other, rather than further apart. We know we're doing this well when we're able to "rejoice with those who rejoice" and "mourn with those who mourn." We can respond with empathy by asking great questions.

Many problems can creep into a relationship because we use personalization instead of empathy. When we personalize something, we expect that another person's bad mood, action, or words are an attack on us, or that we caused them, or are responsible to fix them. I (Ally) had to retrain myself in this area with Jeremy, and work to not take things personally. For example, maybe Jeremy came home and I perceived he was not talkative, or sharing much about his day. Instead of being empathic, supportive, accepting, and understanding of his humanity and low energy, I tended to start to make it...about me.

This was out of fear, mostly, and the result was never good. I would start to worry if I was doing something wrong, or if he was unhappy with me, etc. It was as if I thought him just being tired was not possible, that it had to be about me. The same thing can happen if someone is angry, or has any other uncomfortable emotion. If they try to make us responsible for the emotion, or if we allow ourselves to feel responsible for that emotion,

78

we will lack health in our relationship. It is not our emotion to resolve, but we can help support them in finding a resolution.

Empathy requires us to take the focus off ourselves and actively listen to the other person, with the goal to understand their perspective. It means resisting the temptation to talk about ourselves. When someone is communicating with us, they're giving us vital information about what they're experiencing. Adopting the goal of empathy means to put yourself in the backseat of the conversation, and focus on picking up every clue we can about what's going for them in the conversation. When we do this, we discover more about who they are and they will feel closer to us, and safer sharing.

What we're looking for is simple, so simple all we need to do is ask them two questions: what do they see is going on, and what do they need? We do not need to agree with their views or needs, because all of us are wired differently. But, if we can demonstrate that we understand what they see and address what they need, we have an avenue to pursue connections with them. We're then able to lower the fear in the conversation and help them resolve things relationally and emotionally. Empathy becomes a vital tool in building a strong relationship.

❖

Prayer

*God, thank You that empathy is at the very core of who You are!
You always know exactly how I feel, and always meet me where I'm at.
I'm so grateful for my relationship with You and I want to express empathy
in the same way to others. With You, I know I can go deep with people to truly hear
and understand them, and ensure that they feel valued and cared for with me,
just as I always feel with You. I know that Your love is always increasing in me.
Let it show how I love people. I can develop empathy by choosing to listen to the needs
of others. I commit to making understanding my goal when I'm communicating
with others so that they will feel heard, cared for, and understood by me.*

Reflection

1. Choose a story from scripture, and start by asking yourself what each person in the story might have been thinking, feeling, or needing.

   _____

   _____

   _____

   _____

2. How easy do you find it to access empathy in conversations with people close to you?

   _____

   _____

   _____

   _____

3. How can you tell when somebody is being empathetic toward you?

   _____

   _____

   _____

   _____

4. How does this impact the connection and strength of the relationship?

   _____

   _____

   _____

   _____

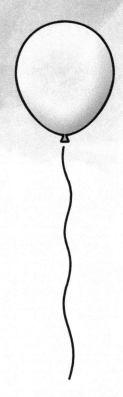

Day 17 – Ownership

MOVING TOWARD
EACH OTHER

*"What if every moment of conflict is a chance to make your
relationship even stronger?"*

Crismarie Campbell

"Therefore, if you bring your gift to the altar, and there remember that your brother has something against you, leave your gift there before the altar, and go your way. First be reconciled to your brother, and then come and offer your gift."

Matthew 5:23-24

Times of relational disagreement or conflict can be hard to navigate. When we're hurt, our instinct is often to hide, run away, or lash out. Sometimes we wonder if we still want to be in the relationship at all. But when we understand God's heart for relationships and commit to that, these times of pressure need not be scary or feel like "deal breakers," in fact, they are actually times we may receive an upgrade if we remain openhearted!

We glimpse God's priority for connection in Matthew 5. Jesus tells us that if we're mid-conflict with another person, we should resolve that conflict before we offer our worship to God. He is asking that we try to restore connection with each other when there's been a disagreement or conflict. He tells us to move toward those who have something against us, even when it's hard. He knows that when we create distance with each other, we're ultimately trying to stay safe, but this strategy will only cause unhappiness. He's asking us to be brave, to be the one to keep our heart open and loving, because love has the power to cover and resolve a multitude of issues.

One way to bridge the gap between fear and love is through a posture of openness and curiosity. When you're tempted to move away from someone, or notice them moving away from you, ask questions. Was the thing they said intended to be hurtful, or were they trying to express something in their heart? Could your interpretation of events differ from theirs? Could they be feeling equally hurt and misunderstood? When we stay committed to asking questions, often we can get to a breakthrough of deeper awareness and understanding.

We all know the heartbreaking story of Adam and Eve after they'd eaten from the forbidden tree, hiding beneath their fig leaves from God. They chose distance and separation out of shame, but God continued to move toward them even in the moment of their greatest betrayal. "Where are you?" He asked curiously (though we know He already knew). He then put in an elaborate plan to restore what they lost in that moment for humankind—connection to Him. You and I are part of that plan! God never stops moving toward us, and we get to be like Him in this way, too. When we realize God's priority for relationships, we can take responsibility for the relationships in our lives. We can then obey Jesus's instruction to keep moving toward each other regardless of what's going on and commit to seeking the knowledge and skills necessary to do this.

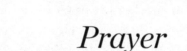

Prayer

God, thank You for moving toward me in love no matter what.
Thank You for revealing Your love to others by choosing to move toward them in love even when it's hard. Enlarge my heart as I fearlessly demonstrate this kind of love to those around me. No matter how I feel, drive me to move toward You and those you love. With Your love, I can climb mountains to pursue You. Show me the clear path and straight way to move toward connection.

Reflection

1. Are there times when you have experienced a conflict starting due to a misunderstanding?

   _____

   _____

   _____

   _____

2. How might curiosity instead of assumption have prevented conflict in that situation?

   _____

   _____

   _____

   _____

3. Are there any people right now you need to resolve a conflict with?

   _____

   _____

   _____

   _____

4. How does (or might) it impact your relationship with God when you know you imitated Christ in conflict resolution?

   _____

   _____

   _____

   _____

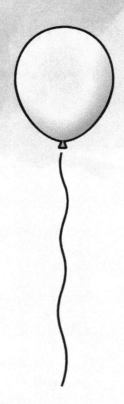

Day 18 – Openness

CHOOSING LOVE OVER RUNNING AWAY

*"Life with God is not immunity from difficulties,
but peace in difficulties."*

C. S. Lewis

"And the peace of God, which surpasses all understanding, will guard your hearts and minds through Christ Jesus."

Philippians 4:7

At first glance, it is easy to see the logic in avoiding emotional pain. Who wants to get hurt? Nobody! All of us have experienced some kind of relational pain. We often adjust our behavior based on our previous experiences, and this is part of being human. It serves a purpose—to protect us. Fleeing may be the right response to all kinds of danger, but in relationships, it stops us moving forward into healthy experiences of love. When we recognize that flight is a fear-based reaction, we can choose new responses that draw us into the deep relationships we desire.

In Philippians, we are promised that the peace of God that surpasses our understanding is available to us, to fill our hearts and minds. This is important because we make very different decisions from a place of peace than we do from a place of fear. When we always fall back on emotionally or physically fleeing in relationships, this leads to loneliness, relational disconnection, and increased fear. At the core of this problem is a lack of trust in yourself and a lack of confidence that you are going to be okay. But here is the good news: you have made it through every painful thing in your life so far. You will continue to make it through.

When we are emotionally triggered, the most important step is to take ownership and find out what we need to calm ourselves down. A healthier version of running away is taking an intentional break to understand what is needed, and then return to the conversion. As we run from fear, we also run away from solutions, leaving us feeling overwhelmed by all the unresolved problems. You get to choose how you will respond to the pain you experience in relationships. You get to choose if it makes things worse and creates compounding bad fruit, or if you cut off the bad fruit and focus on moving forward. The perfect love of God can heal and sustain us even when people let us down, reject us, or hurt us.

We love what Moses says to God in Exodus 33. God offers to send an angel with the Israelites to take them into the promised land, but Moses says "No way! If you're not going, I'm not going." Being with God was more important to him than getting to the promised land. His highest value was to stay connected to God. When we adopt this as our highest value, it will impact our responses in our relationship with others too. Today, let peace be your guide as you choose your responses in relationships.

Prayer

*God, thank You that you see the patterns of my past and they
don't scare You at all! You can't wait to reveal to me Your new patterns,
and watch me flourish as I learn Your ways. I'm thankful for Your abundant,
empowering grace that always leads me into life. Why would I run away
when I can run into love? You already know every good gift you have for me
in relationships. I can't wait to see every fear overcome by love in my life!
I love You, Jesus.*

Reflection

1. Do you feel the urge to run when conversations get hard?

    _____

    _____

    _____

    _____

2. What kind of topics or behaviors are most likely to trigger
    this behavior?

    _____

    _____

    _____

    _____

3. What would it take for you to stay in a hard conversation?

    _____

    _____

    _____

    _____

4. How could you help someone else feel safe enough to stay in a
    hard conversation?

    _____

    _____

    _____

    _____

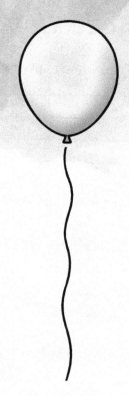

Day 19 – Ownership

FEARLESS
RELATIONSHIPS

"Courage is not the absence of fear, but rather the assessment that something else is more important than fear."

Franklin D. Roosevelt

"Have I not commanded you?
Be strong and courageous. Do not be afraid;
do not be discouraged, for the Lord your God
will be with you wherever you go. "

Joshua 1:9 NIV

Imagine what would change if you became fearless in your relationships? God is fearless in connecting with you. His desire is that you imitate Him by becoming fearless in how you love. No matter what your relationship history has been, it is the priority of your heavenly father to love you so abundantly that it displaces every fear in your life. He wants to be your source, your oasis, and your teacher in relationships. Then you will become a walking demonstration of love to those around you.

In Joshua 1:9, God tells Joshua to be strong and courageous in pursuing the Promised Land. The reason He gives for this strength and courage is simple: "for I will be with you." God knows that His presence is the antidote to fear. He promises never to withhold this, not from Joshua, and not from you. Joshua is about to embark on one the most important journeys of his life—pursuing the land God had ordained for the Israelites to possess. In the same way, there is a promised land that God has ordained for you in relationships, and to go after it means choosing courage and fearlessly pursuing what's yours.

Fear can have devastating effects on relationships. When we operate out of fear, our instinct is to self-protect. Our instinct is to stop taking ownership for ourselves and instead blame others. We create distance, and ultimately sow disconnection from others. Each of our actions creates a kind of soil for our relationships to grow in. They create healthy, rich, vibrant relationships, or dull, struggling relationships. How we respond to fear impacts that soil. It is worth the work to remove fear from the soil.

Part of how we do this is by resolving fears in ourselves, instead of expecting others to be responsible for doing this. Notice this verse does not say, "I will command others to stop doing or saying things that cause you fear." No, God focuses on Joshua and helps him create a better process of removing fear from his life. When we resolve our fear of rejection, or being misunderstood, we take pressure off the relationship to fix the fear. We take ownership for the fear. We are committed to understanding ourselves, and we share that with each other from a place of strength, not fear. When we're strong and courageous, and partner with the spirit of love, He displaces fear and sets our course toward healthy, happy relationships.

✦

Prayer

God, thank You that perfect love casts out all fear! As You fill me with Your perfect love, I naturally become fearless in my relationships. I choose to partner with fearlessness as I pursue connection that lowers fear and creates safety. When I walk into Your love, the fear lets go of my heart and mind. I am able to accomplish all that You place in me because of Your spirit of love that empowers me. Jesus, will You bring forth the fearlessness of God in my life like a mighty wind? I seek Your strength and courage to move me.

Reflection

1. If you woke up tomorrow and a miracle happened where you no longer had any fear in your relationships, what would be different in your day, conversations, and thoughts?

   _____

   _____

   _____

   _____

2. What are the relational fears that need to be cast out or replaced with God's love in your life?

   _____

   _____

   _____

   _____

3. Is there a specific relationship in your life where fear has caused disconnection?

   _____

   _____

   _____

   _____

4. What might the "promised land" in this relationship look like?

   _____

   _____

   _____

   _____

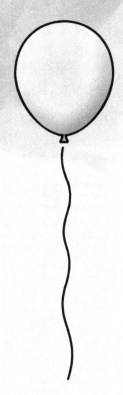

Day 20 – Openness

CHOOSING LOVE OVER FIGHTING BACK

"If this is to be achieved, man must evolve for all human conflict a method which rejects revenge, aggression, and retaliation. The foundation of such a method is love."

Martin Luther King, Jr.

"No one has seen God at any time.
If we love one another, God abides in us,
and His love has been perfected in us."

1 John 4:12 NKJV

J ust like choosing to run or hide, choosing to fight can be an instinctive fear-based reaction when we're scared. So, how do we choose love instead? 1 John 4:12 says, "No one has ever seen God, but if we love one another, God lives in us, and His love is made complete in us." This is encouraging because it tells us that it's not by our power alone but by the love of God within us that we're able to change.

It might feel powerful to stamp and roar like a lion during a conversation, but it's actually a powerless, self-protective response that aims to control others. It takes no strength to be overtaken by an emotion that creates destruction in our lives and relationships. It makes you powerless. It communicates one loud message: "I matter and you don't, and if you try to matter, I'll shut you down!" Most people who react in this way when they're scared don't realize that this is the message they're sending. When we invite the love of God to transform our hearts and minds, we can learn new responses to fear, miscommunication, and problems.

When I (Jeremy) was about ten, I had a revelation that anger did not actually tend to solve things. I would observe people yelling at each other at school, or during sports, and what I realized was that it rarely had a positive effect or led to change. It was about one person's lack of control over their emotions more than it was about a solution. People who were angry seemed to be going in circles of anger instead of resolving anything. I even got so bold to tell some people, "Do you think that is really helping you?" Normally, they responded poorly to this and felt I was a smart aleck, but no one could show me evidence of it being helpful, so it was never a communication strategy I developed. Instead, when we choose to listen, understand, and get to the root of the problem, we reinforce the truth that we value the relationship. With the love of God, every fear can be transformed by truth!

Prayer

God, thank You that Your love is the antidote to fear, and I love more of it than I can handle! Continue to pour Your love into me so I can be transformed more and more into the image of Your son. I don't want to fight back any more; I want to create an atmosphere of love everywhere I go. I know because You abide in me, this is more than possible; it's highly likely! Thank You for the healing You've already done in my heart, and the great freedom You created me to live in.

Reflection

1. How does it impact your relationship when you are confronted with the T-Rex behavior of others?

   _____

   _____

   _____

   _____

2. Is fighting back a typical response for you in some situations more than others?

   _____

   _____

   _____

   _____

3. What do you fear might happen if you are not loud and aggressive in your reaction?

   _____

   _____

   _____

   _____

4. Find a key scripture you can repeat to yourself to help remind you to stay calm when you are tempted to react.

   _____

   _____

   _____

   _____

Day 21 – Ownership

EVERYTHING MEANINGFUL TAKES HARD WORK

"You don't develop courage by being happy in your relationships every day. You develop it by surviving difficult times and challenging adversity."

Epicurus

*"Two are better than one;
because they have a good reward for their labor.
For if they fall, the one will lift up his fellow."*

Ecclesiastes 4:9-10 NKJV

earning to think about relationships differently and become effective at using new tools and strategies doesn't happen overnight, but like with most things, practice makes perfect. It's actually a comfort to know that quality relationships don't just happen by accident. This means they're available to everyone, not just a lucky few who "happen" to find each other.

It is God's desire that we learn how to do relationships well, so that two may truly be better than one, as described in Ecclesiastes 4. Great relationships are a blessing to the people in them. This verse tells us "they have a good reward for their labor. For if they fall, the one will lift up his fellow... Though one may be overpowered by another, two can withstand him." It is my view that not every relationship is a blessing in this way. To receive the blessings intended for relationships takes intentionality and effort.

Lifelong love might be the desire of every couple on their wedding day, or every new parent, but to achieve that goal always takes a choice to work on the relationship. In fact, it's a lot like working out at the gym. You might want a great body, or to run a marathon, but to reach that goal requires showing up, working out, and coming back the next day. We build healthy relationships the same way—through hard work. The first step is finding the relational tools and strategies that will build connection, and then practicing them until they become established.

Have you noticed that Jesus seldom seems in a hurry in the Bible? His disciples don't "get" everything straightaway; they make mistakes, try to rush toward instant results, and get it wrong. He's trying to help them adopt a kingdom mindset, but it takes time. Jesus rebukes James and John for suggesting they call down fire on a Samaritan village. Jesus has to restore a soldier's ear because Peter chops it off. He didn't expect them to get it right away—but as they kept showing up and walking with Him, they became established in a whole new way of thinking, one that would ultimately cause them to change the world. Jesus is walking with you as you learn these new tools and apply the hard work that leads to great fruit. Keep showing up, and do not give up! The intimacy experiences you crave are within your reach.

Prayer

God, thank You for designing me to work hard and be fruitful.
I know that successful relationships take effort, but it's always worth it.
I commit to working hard at being open and taking ownership, so that my relationships can flourish. God, You are such a good role model for hard work. You create and recreate day and night on my behalf, working to bring our dreams together.
I want to be like Jesus, always working to be about the Father's business.
Show me the rewards of work just as You see them.
Thank You, Jesus.

Reflection

1. What motivates you to persevere when things get tough?
    What do you need to know?

    _____

    _____

    _____

    _____

2. Are you generally good at rewarding yourself when you work hard
    to reach your goals?

    _____

    _____

    _____

    _____

3. How good are you at celebrating successes and moving
    past failures?

    _____

    _____

    _____

    _____

4. How does kindness to yourself help you to achieve your goals?

    _____

    _____

    _____

    _____

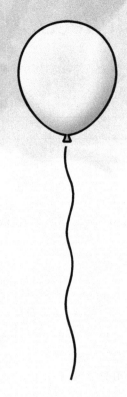

Day 22 – Openness

LEARNING THE
LANGUAGES OF LOVE

"In the New Testament, love is more of a verb than a noun.
It has more to do with acting than with feeling. The call to love
is not so much a call to a certain state of feeling
as it is to a quality of action."

R. C. Sproul

"Dear children, let us not love with words or speech but with actions and in truth. This is how we know that we belong to the truth and how we set our hearts at rest in His presence."

1 John 3:18-19 NIV

We're always sending and receiving messages in relationships, and we're always either moving toward each other or away from each other. Recognizing that people receive love in different ways, and finding out what those are, gives us the information we need to keep moving toward each other. This is the reason we like Gary Chapman's book The Five Languages (though, respectfully, we would say there are limitless ways to express love even within those categories, and we think there are more than five languages). This book talks about how different we all are and gives us some great tools to love each other regardless of those differences. As people who pursue the goal of connection, it is full of valuable tools to move toward each other in our closest relationships.

Have you ever felt like somebody was missing the mark in how they tried to show you love? Have you ever felt like you're pouring affection on someone, but it doesn't seem to get through to them at all? That's because we all love differently, and when we figure out how the people around us give and receive love, we're able to offer and receive love in meaningful ways. Once we know how to love a person according to their love language, we have power in our hands! We can move toward them by offering them love in this way, even if it doesn't come naturally to us, or we can use this knowledge to withhold love from them and create an even greater distance. When we take responsibility for this choice and choose to offer love, we build connection and trust in our relationships.

Knowing someone's love language tells you how to make deposits into their love bank account and keep it full of resources. When people have lots of withdrawals coming out of their account (stress, fear, frustration, disconnection, giving to others) and no deposits, they feel depleted and unhappy. Our goal in moving toward each other is to make sure we are making regular deposits. Jesus showed love to different people in different ways depending on who they were, what their history was, and what they needed, specifically. He didn't superimpose one kind of love. True love is about putting aside our need to love a certain way and instead give what is needed based on the other person's needs. 1 John 3:18-19 reminds us that our love is proven not just in our words but our actions and in truth. When we love people selflessly, and act accordingly, we are showing this kind of love.

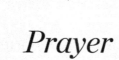

Prayer

God, thank You for creating each of your children to be unique. You know just how to reach our hearts, and how to love us in the language we best understand. As I pursue healthy relationships, I love that I can take responsibility for finding out how others give and receive love, actively pursue this, and send great messages that communicate "I love you" just how they can best receive it. I'm so grateful to be able to partner with You in showing love to the people around me in meaningful ways!

Reflection

1. Write about the various ways God has shown love to you. Think of as many as you can!

   _____

   _____

   _____

   _____

2. Now, do a bit of research in the Bible! How did God show love to others in the Bible?

   _____

   _____

   _____

   _____

3. Finally, think of others. How have you seen others show love?

   _____

   _____

   _____

   _____

4. Of everything you have written so far, which ways of showing love can you continue to grow in personally?

   _____

   _____

   _____

   _____

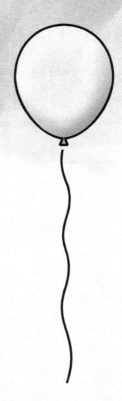

Day 23– Ownership

ESTABLISHING A STRONG CONNECTION

*"If we knew how much God loved us and was for us,
we'd talk to Him all day long"*

Donald Miller

*"Set me as a seal upon your heart,
As a seal upon your arm; For love is as strong
as death, Jealousy as cruel as the grave; Its flames are
flames of fire, A most vehement flame."*

Song of Songs 8:6 NKJV

When we live in the revelation of God's passionate love for us, know that the plumb-line for all connection is our connection with Him. He is a father; He is a friend, and He is a passionate lover of our souls. Song of Songs invites us into the beauty of Jesus's heart for His bride, and we can continuously respond to His unrelenting love in our lives. God's number one goal is connection with us. And He is our model for how to have the best relationships with others. He created us for love and He sent His son to pay the ultimate price to restore connection with us, and no matter how close or how far away He feels, He never stops pursuing this goal. How great is that? Our job is to place God at the center of our lives, and when we do, we can access the peace, comfort, safety, and joy that meets our deepest needs.

Putting God at the center of our lives means recognizing Him as our ultimate source of love. This means relating to God with vulnerability, bringing Him our broken spots, and trusting His perfect love to bring comfort and healing. When we realize that our source of love is always available and unconditional, we relate to others differently. We no longer need them to "fill us up" in unhealthy ways and instead depend on them for the love God designed them to give.

The Psalms give us a great example of a son passionately and vulnerably relating to God. In psalm after psalm, we see David pour his heart out—the good, the bad, and the ugly. We see moments of anger and unbelief, and we see him find faith and hope again. Most of all, we see honesty and vulnerability. David didn't think he needed to "say the right thing"

106

or pretend when he was in the presence of God. He knew that God loved him unconditionally, and his true feelings were not only okay; God wanted to hear them. God valued the truth of what was in His son's heart, and loved to meet him in that place. He loves it when you share honestly with Him too! It is only then you can allow Him to help and comfort you! As we make God our source, and practice sharing our thoughts, feelings, and needs with Him, we not only strengthen our connection with Him; we gain access to boundless spiritual resources to sustain us in moving toward our relationship goals with other people.

Prayer

God, thank You for always being eager to connect to me, even when I am struggling.
My relationship with You is the most precious thing in my life.
My priority is to glorify You in my relationships by listening to what You're saying,
and doing what You're doing and being led by You in all things.
I will always come back to You in the center of my universe.
You are the plumbline of my life, my cornerstone.
Show me how You are at the center of each and every dream in my heart.
Thank You for bringing me closer to You.

Reflection

1. Consider in scripture all the times God loved, provided, encouraged, and comforted despite people sharing vulnerable feelings.

   _____

   _____

   _____

   _____

2. Journal today the truth of what you feel, especially hard or conflicted feelings.

   _____

   _____

   _____

   _____

3. Whether you feel your journal entry is good, bad, or ugly, accept that God wants to meet you in the truth where He can love and support you.

   _____

   _____

   _____

   _____

4. Review your journal entry and ask God His thoughts and desires for you.

   _____

   _____

   _____

   _____

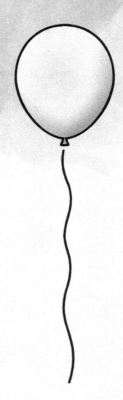

Day 24~ Openness

LETTING GO
OF BEING RIGHT

"It's more important to be kind than to be right."

Bianca Olthoff

"Love is patient and kind; love does not envy or boast; it is not arrogant or rude. It does not insist on its own way..."

1 Corinthians 13:4-5 ESV

It's never fun to get stuck in a place of disagreement where both people think they're right! We all have opinions and views, and expressing and debating them is part of human nature. Unfortunately, being right often becomes so important to us it overtakes the goal of having a healthy relationship. Needing to be right or win an argument makes us feel like we're on opposite teams, instead of the same one. When we remember that our highest priority is a healthy relationship with each other, we can make space for differing opinions. 1 Corinthians 13:4-5 tells us that love is not only patient and kind, but it "does not insist on its own way." This tells us that the need to be right is not compatible with love!

Needing to be right robs our relationship's potential. When we make our partner our opponent, we forget not only whose team we're on; we forget what game we're playing! Winning the wrong game can leave us feeling empty and unsatisfied. Sure, maybe we won the argument, but if a friend is feeling misunderstood and unheard, we've lost connection. In every relationship, the ultimate goal is staying connected. If we remember this, it doesn't really matter who wins, but that both people felt loved and stayed committed to finding a way forward together. It's not always easy, but keeping our priorities right means we can say, "Sure, we're different. But you get to be you, and I get to be me in this relationship." When our opinions differ, we can start to move toward connection by asking questions like, "What do you need?" and "How can I help you with that?" to facilitate connection instead of arguing.

Jesus purposely created opportunities for His followers to prioritize connection above offense, confusion, and agreement. He knew that they would need practice if they were to protect their connection until the end! One example of this is when He did something the Jews considered wrong, and healed a man on the Sabbath (Mark 3). Connection and healing were more important than being right in the Jew's eyes. The disciples then went on to change the world! Imagine the offense they needed to get over when Paul arrived on the scene, announcing that the message reserved for the Jews was for the Gentiles too? Imagine Peter's surprise when he was told in a vision to kill and eat, when eating unclean meat had been considered wrong for centuries. The disciples had to learn to choose connection above their perception of what was right at the time. We can do the same, and if we do, we'll avoid the snares that would trip us up. We can have relationships of peace where we feel deeply connected.

Prayer

God, thank You that as I make connection a higher priority than being right, I can change my approach to disagreements. I choose to set a new standard in my relationships. Thank You that Your peace is always available to me as I forge new paths of healthy communication in my relationships. I accept Your peace in my times of uncertainty and embrace the hug of Your love when I don't have all the answers. Guide me down the path of always seeing the main priority in relationships: love. Show me where love can abound and teach me how to grow it. Thank You, Jesus!

Reflection

1. Does your inner critic value you being right or wrong more than connection with yourself and others?

    _____

    _____

    _____

    _____

2. Do any fears come up when you think of not fighting to be "right" but fighting instead for connection?

    _____

    _____

    _____

    _____

3. What tone, behavior, or language might you need to change in order to communicate connection?

    _____

    _____

    _____

    _____

4. Write a vision statement for your goal in navigating "right and wrong" in relationships.

    _____

    _____

    _____

    _____

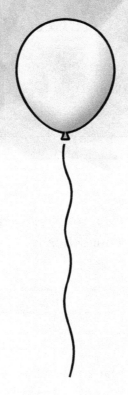

RESPONDING
WITH COMPASSION

"Between stimulus and response there is a space. In that space is our power to choose our response. In our response lies our growth and our freedom."

Victor Frankl

"But you, Lord, are a compassionate and gracious God, slow to anger, abounding in love and faithfulness."

Psalm 86:15 NIV

How easy do you find it to access compassion amid difficult situations? Most of us find this tough, but there are some great strategies we can learn to access peace and compassion. Psalm 86 tells us that God is "compassionate and gracious...slow to anger, abounding in love and faithfulness." And guess what? You were made in His image! That means you have everything you need to learn to respond with compassion and graciousness, too!

Reactions are one of the biggest things that get in the way of compassion. They are often quick responses, which we may regret later. In the heat of the moment, we say the first thing that comes to mind, rather than thoughtfully choosing our words. People who take ownership know that quick reactions can create distance and pain. Responding is a choice to fully own how we act and show up in a relationship, and do our best to keep our actions from causing pain. We can all train our minds to pause when we feel a reaction rising within us, remind ourselves of our priorities, and choose a response instead. Taking "response-ability" is what protects relationships from unnecessary pain and builds healthy connections.

Learning to pause before we react is the simplest step toward the goal of learning to respond. We can start when we notice our thoughts and body during hard conversations. Do you feel shaky? Does your heart beat faster? Learn what your early warning signs are and use these as a signal to take five deep breaths, take a time out, or drink a glass of water. Recognize and accept the compassion God has for you in that moment of struggle. Focus on what you need to regain control of your emotion and composure. Say something compassionate to yourself like, "You are doing great." "This is stressful, but you'll be okay." "It is fine to feel frustrated, but also make a healthy choice."

By creating the space for compassion and empathy for ourselves, we can show compassion toward others. We can recognize they don't want to be judged by their mistakes or wrongs, and they crave our grace and understanding. We can each take responsibility for our part in building healthy and connected relationships. Jesus shows this beautifully. When the woman caught in adultery was brought to Him, He didn't react in anger, either to her or the people who brought her. He paused, drew in the sand, and waited. He thought out his response, which was challenging and yet full of compassion, and diffused a conflict. We can do this too if we get good at responding, rather than reacting.

Prayer

God, thank You that we see compassion demonstrated time and again in the life of Jesus. As I spend time with people today, fill me with Your compassion. I choose to see with Your eyes and listen with Your ears so that I can accept and then demonstrate Your heart today. Your compassion moves You into releasing so many miracles. It is incredible to see compassion lived out. I glean from You in my relationships to extend compassion through love to bring about the outcomes of Your will. Thank You that compassion is available for me because of You.

Reflection

1. What are behaviors and words you have seen others use in a reaction versus a response?

   _____

   _____

   _____

   _____

2. What signals does your body send you when you are starting to feel a reaction?

   _____

   _____

   _____

   _____

3. What is something you can say to yourself as encouragement to be more compassionate to yourself?

   _____

   _____

   _____

   _____

4. Describe the impact it will have on your relationships if others feel you respond with compassion instead of reacting? (e.g., will they trust you more, be honest more, feel safer with you, feel more loving toward you?)

   _____

   _____

   _____

   _____

Day 26– Openness

GIFTS ARE
A WAY TO LOVE

"It's not how much we give but how much love we put into giving."

Mother Theresa

"Every good and perfect gift is from above, coming down from the Father of the heavenly lights, who does not change like shifting shadows."

James 1:17 NIV

Gifts have been an important part of our culture for centuries. They're often used to commemorate big moments like weddings, births, and even deaths. When Jesus was born, the wise men showed their honor for who He was by bringing the rare and precious gifts of gold, frankincense, and myrrh. There was no natural reason to bring a baby born in a stable such things. The gifts in themselves conveyed meaning. They said, "We see you. We recognize who you are—messiah and future king." The gifts affirmed Jesus's identity as it had been revealed to them by God.

For some people, gifts are their primary love language. If you take the time to think about them, and buy something thoughtful and meaningful, they feel known and loved. Likewise, they love to spend hours choosing the perfect gift for others, writing a card, and seeing the look on their face when it's opened! "Gifts" people are looking for evidence that the people in their lives know them and think about them, even when they're not with them, and they love to do this for others, too. For them, the gift is the evidence they need that you're holding them close to your heart.

Luckily, for "gifts" people, it's not about how big or expensive the gift is. In fact, I'm sure the person who invented the saying "it's the thought that counts" was a "gifts" person! So, there is no need to feel pressure. A meaningful gift could be something as simple as some flowers or a cupcake. It's not about the money spent on the gift, but how much the gift communicates "I know you," or, "I noticed you were going through something." It's this "being remembered" that brings their heart alive. If

118

you know people like this, chances are you've been on the receiving end of some great gifts, too!

Meaningful, thoughtful gifts can be a great way to affirm the identity of the people in your life, and show them you know, appreciate, and love them. James 1:17 tells us that every good gift comes from heaven! We know that the Father loves to give good gifts to His children. In the same way, let's be great at giving good gifts to each other, recognizing that it's an age-old way of showing love and honor.

———————— ✦ ————————

Prayer

God, thank You for giving good gifts to Your children.
Where my spouse, friends, or family are "gifts" people,
I commit to finding creative ways to love them in this way.
Thank You that You're with me as I look for inspiration to choose great gifts,
knowing they carry weight for the person who is receiving them.
Holy Spirit, I look forward to the treasure hunts we will go on together
to find tokens of love that will speak into the hearts of those I love!
I'm grateful that You, Father, are the greatest gift giver!

Reflection

1. How comfortable are you with giving and receiving love through gifts?

   _____

   _____

   _____

   _____

2. Do you know anyone who is really good at loving through gifts?

   _____

   _____

   _____

   _____

3. What might you be able to do to better show love through gift-giving?

   _____

   _____

   _____

   _____

4. On your calendar, write down a date and a way you can practice showing love to someone by giving a gift.

   _____

   _____

   _____

   _____

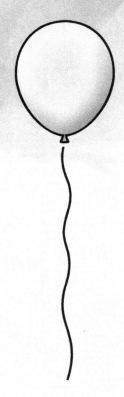

Day 27 – Ownership

THE CHOICE
TO LOVE

"If you do fall in love, make sure you make a covenant to grow in love, because what began as an accident needs to be done on purpose!"

Kris Vallotton

"You did not choose me but I chose you, and appointed you that you would go and bear fruit, and that your fruit would remain, so that whatever you ask of the Father in my name He may give to you"

John 15:16 NKJV

Relational health isn't random, but based on our choice to take full ownership of the quantity and quality of the love we give. "I choose you" is the foundation of true, lasting relationships. It's the heart of the marriage vow, the deep friendship, and even family relationships. Most importantly, it's also the foundation for God's relationship with you! Jesus said to His disciples, "You did not choose me, but I chose you." Jesus chose you during the hardest circumstances, when you were in sin and His enemy. He made His choice, and no matter what you do, He does not change His mind.

Jesus's side of the relationship doesn't depend on your choice, but entirely on His choice. The question is, will you follow His example and build your relationships with others on the foundation of your choice? A healthy relationship can only be built between two people who choose each other and take full responsibility for that choice. A choice is an act of the will. It is not dependent on feelings, someone's behavior, or circumstances. When two people understand that the other has committed to choosing them no matter what, they're not only free to be themselves; they feel safe to communicate their needs, desires, and boundaries, and this creates the best environment for a relationship to thrive.

Jesus chose each of His disciples, inviting them to leave everything to follow Him, and each of them agreed. He chose them, and they chose Him. It rarely costs much to make an initial choice to love another person. There is something even more wonderful about our choice to continue to love when it feels hard. But actually, this is one of the highest callings we can attain in life. This deep love that focuses on what it can give more than what it can get. We would argue that these moments of love demonstrate an imitation of Jesus more than being a missionary or starting a mega church. In John 6, the disciples may have realized that following Jesus wasn't always going to be easy. Jesus turned to the twelve and said, "Do you also want to go away?" They answered in the spirit of "No! We still choose you." Choosing to love repeatedly creates the environment in which we all thrive in relationships.

Prayer

God, thank You that I am Your chosen! Thank You for creating me to thrive in relationships in which I've been chosen, committed to, and loved unconditionally. Thank You that I don't have to "fall" into relationships, but I get to choose who I choose and who I let choose me. Thank You for this choice of love. I want to walk out my pursuit with those You have given me in my relationships. They are my chosen and You support me in loving them even when times are hard. You always choose to love. Thank You, Jesus.

Reflection

1. In what ways has God demonstrated to you that you are chosen by Him to be loved?

_____

_____

_____

_____

2. Is anything getting in the way of you choosing God in return?

_____

_____

_____

_____

3. Is there anything that tends to get in the way of you consistently demonstrating your commitment to those you have chosen? (e.g., changing feelings, offence, anger, avoidance, etc.)

_____

_____

_____

_____

4. How can you overcome anything getting in the way of your commitment to choose God and others?

_____

_____

_____

_____

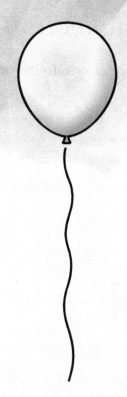

Day 28– Openness

EXPERIENCING UNCONDITIONAL LOVE

"The strength of a good friendship that goes the distance will be unconditional love."

Brian Houston

"And I am convinced that nothing can ever separate us from God's love. Neither death nor life, neither angels nor demons, neither our fears for today nor our worries about tomorrow—not even the powers of hell can separate us from God's love. No power in the sky above or in the earth below—indeed, nothing in all creation will ever be able to separate us from the love of God that is revealed in Christ, Jesus our Lord."

Romans 8:38-39 NKJV

Is your deepest desire to be loved unconditionally? If so, you're not alone! This is how God created us, and He shows this to us every day in our relationship with Him. Romans 8 tells us that nothing can separate us from the love of God! "Neither death nor life, neither angels nor demons, neither our fears for today nor our worries about tomorrow—not even the powers of hell can separate us from God's love." That's pretty unconditional! God's design for us is to thrive in unconditional love, and He has a plan for us to experience this in our relationship with Him and others.

Not only is unconditional love an attainable standard for our relationships with others; it's in fact a prerequisite for healthy, happy relationships. We build intimacy layer by layer as we learn to trust each other. Many relational problems happen because we're struggling to trust, or because we are focusing on what we can get more than what we can give. For a relationship to be healthy, there must be a balance of give and take in both directions. When there is, it develops trust. No human relationship is perfect. Our Father God is our perfect source of unconditional love, and He is able to provide us with unconditional love without measure, love that we can depend on to fill the gaps when those around us are unable to do this. We can step into God's design for relationships when we come to them with an approach of "more than enough."

Peter denied Jesus three times just before His crucifixion. He demonstrated his humanity and that his love was conditional. This must

126

have been devastating for Peter and Jesus. The amazing thing is that when they next meet, Peter sees Jesus on the beach and runs toward Him. Jesus gives Peter the opportunity to redeem his denial of Him by getting him to declare his love for Him three times. They don't pull back; they keep moving toward each other. This is love, and what Peter lacked, Jesus redeemed and restored. He wants to do the same for you. Where can you give someone an opportunity to meet your needs? In the same way, think about someone in your life who has expressed a need to you. How can you build trust between you by meeting their needs?

✦

Prayer

God, thank You that Your love is unconditional.
No matter what I do or don't do, You freely give Your love to me.
In the same way, I choose to freely give my love to others today.
I choose not to withhold love based on somebody's words or actions.
Your love is incredible. It is a force that creates millions of wonderful moments.
Nothing keeps Your love away. I want to display my love like you do.
Allow Your unconditional love to flow through me to those I love.
Show me how to keep the gates of my heart open all the time.
Thank You, Jesus!

Reflection

1. Write down a few sentences explaining what unconditional love means to you.

    _____

    _____

    _____

    _____

2. Where have you experienced unconditional love in your life? Where is it easiest for you to show it?

    _____

    _____

    _____

    _____

3. Is there anything you fear might separate you from the love, value, or blessing of God? What would He say about this?

    _____

    _____

    _____

    _____

4. How can you grow toward meeting the expressed needs of others in relationships? What would you need in order to grow toward expressing more of your needs in the relationships?

    _____

    _____

    _____

    _____

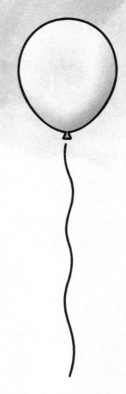

Day 29– Ownership

THE JOY OF
SELF-CONTROL

"Control and manipulation are not love; the outcome is a life of imprisonment ultimately leading to deep-rooted feelings of resentment."

Ken Poirot

*"Better a patient person than a warrior,
one with self-control than one who takes a city."*

Proverbs 16:32 NIV

The fruits of the spirit are able to help guide us and our relationships into powerful places. One of these fruits is self-control. Self-control is a wonderful thing! Not mentioned in the list of fruits of the spirit is control of others. When we feel out of control or fear the loss of our own control, we look to control things outside of ourselves. The tools of powerlessness seek to control, manipulate, remove freedom, threaten, and withhold love. Proverbs 16:32 says, "Better a patient person than a warrior, one with self-control than one who takes a city." Becoming great at self-control introduces power and freedom into our lives and into the lives of those around us!

Many of us experienced being controlled growing up, and so our natural response is to exert this same control on others. Many parents instill the message: "It's my job to control you. You don't let me control you, then I will introduce pain to teach you that lesson." I'm not talking about parents protecting their children from harm or introducing appropriate consequences for their choices, but parents who believe it's their job to make their children's choices and punish them for making their own choices. Raised in this environment, children learn that if they don't surrender control, the most powerful adult in their life will punish them or withhold love. Ultimately, they will believe the lie that love is about control.

When we repent of the lie that we can control other people, we break the cycle of fear, control, punishment, and disconnection. Developing self-control looks like getting in the habit of communicating what you will do, rather than telling others what they should do. In John 21, we see Peter subtly wanting to control Jesus's actions. Pointing at John, he asks, "What about him?" Jesus responds with a statement that invites us all into self-control. "If I want him to remain alive until I return, what is that to you? You follow me." In this statement, Jesus is reminding Peter that he only has control over and responsibility for his own behavior. When we take these steps to letting go of control, we create new patterns in our relationships, where everybody is expected to make their own choices about their lives.

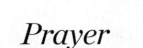

Prayer

God, I fully embrace the joy of self-control! I release the burden of carrying other people and fully settle into the freedom of taking responsibility for my life. I love the freedom that you created each one of us to live in.
I say "yes" to self-control today! God, thank You for giving me the freedom to control my own life. I choose today to imitate You by not trying to control people. I acknowledge the destructive quality of control. I commit to making my relationship a space of freedom, safety, and belonging.

Reflection

1. Are there any areas of your life where fear tempts you to try
   to control others?

   _____

   _____

   _____

   _____

2. What could it practically look like to let this go and only
   control yourself?

   _____

   _____

   _____

   _____

3. In which of your relationships could you practice this?

   _____

   _____

   _____

   _____

4. What would it give you to get really good at only controlling
   yourself?

   _____

   _____

   _____

   _____

Day 30– Openness

TOUCH IS
A WAY TO LOVE

*"Touch is the most basic, the most nonconceptual form
of communication that we have. In touch there are
no language barriers; anything that can walk,
fly, creep, crawl, or swim already speaks it."*

Ina May Gaskin

"His left hand is under my head,
and his right hand embraces me."

Song of Songs 2:8 NKJV

Most often, we are first introduced to people through words and touch by shaking hands. When people are sad, we hug them for comfort. We often offer a pat on the shoulder or a squeeze for reassurance. We hold hands when we feel connected and we draw children close to offer a sense of security. In the Bible, we see Jesus repeatedly heal people through touch, and Paul suggests that impartation of spiritual gifts comes through the laying on of hands. There is no doubt that touch is vitally important to our wellbeing!

Did you know that we are neurobiologically wired to need some level of touch? Touch releases a chemical called oxytocin, which bonds us to others. For some people, however, physical touch is their primary love language. They feel safe, nurtured, and loved when they're getting the touch they need, and agitated if they aren't. It's as if touch people have a touch meter planted inside their chest that connects to every other place in their body like a nerve ending. As the meter is depleted by lack of touch, it registers a higher and higher number of needs. A "touch" person will become increasingly anxious as they become depleted. You'll probably see the worst of them when they feel starved of touch, and the best of them when this need is met.

People who don't like or require touch may find it uncomfortable to meet this need in others. If a "touch" person can communicate his or her needs clearly, without getting anxious, then both parties can move toward one another effectively. If you are not used to giving love through touch, this can feel overwhelming. But you can always start small. Touch can be as

134

simple as a pat on the back, a fist bump, a hug, or a high-five. We get to love people well by recognizing that their need for touch might be greater than ours and offering it as a free gift of love to them.

Prayer

God, thank You for creating our bodies to receive love and comfort through physical touch. This is such an amazing language of love, and one that You wired within each of us to need in a special way. Lord, thank You for the first touch of a mother and child, or the wedding day kiss of a husband and wife. Where my spouse, friends, or family are "physical touch" people, I commit to demonstrating my love for them in this way. I choose to offer touch as a healthy, respectful, and free gift of affection!

Reflection

1. How comfortable are you with giving and receiving love through touch?

    _____

    _____

    _____

    _____

2. Do you know anyone who is really good at loving through healthy physical touch?

    _____

    _____

    _____

    _____

3. What might you learn about "speaking" this love language from observing others who are good at showing love through touch?

    _____

    _____

    _____

    _____

4. On your calendar, write down a date and way you can practice showing love to someone through healthy physical touch.

    _____

    _____

    _____

    _____

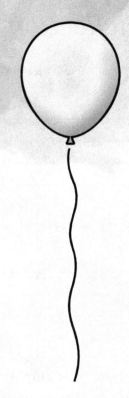

Day 31 – Ownership

GIVING LOVE
AS A FREE GIFT

"Love is always bestowed as a gift—freely, willingly and without expectation. We don't love to be loved. We love to love,"

Leo Buscaglia

"But love your enemies, do good, and lend, hoping for nothing in return; and your reward will be great, and you will be sons of the Most High."

Have you ever wondered why God put two trees in the garden? I have. It would have saved us all a lot of trouble if God had put that tree somewhere out of reach, but He didn't. This is because He wanted a fundamental part of being human to be freedom, and freedom only exists in the presence of choice. Without choice, we don't have freedom, and more importantly, we don't have love, which requires freedom. God is the spirit of love, and to partner with Him we have to offer our love freely based on our choice, not conditioned by what anyone else does or doesn't do.

This is most beautifully expressed by the woman with the Alabaster jar. We read in the gospels that Jesus is sitting at the dinner table when a woman comes in and pours a jar of expensive perfume over His head. We're told that the perfume is probably worth a year's wages—and many of the people at the table are horrified at her "wastefulness." And yet, Jesus is deeply moved by her choice to offer this free gift of love, and honors her by declaring that wherever the gospel is told, her story will be as well. Isn't it great to know that we can offer the same free acts of love, to Jesus and to others?

Once we accept that we can't control others, it's like stepping out of a complicated maze into the wide-open space of freedom. The problem with controlling others is that it is hard work, and work that never ends. Rarely do we feel we are seeing the fruit of all our effort. Instead, we get to see the fruit of learning to control ourselves, our emotions, and our mindsets. This starts as we take steps to remove any barrier that keeps us from receiving God's love for ourselves. As we get better at receiving this free gift, with no strings attached, we get better at giving it.

Luke 6:35 encourages us to love our enemies, to do good and lend, hoping for nothing in return. In God's kingdom, we need not withhold love from anybody or try to control them, because we have a never-ending source of love pouring into us, and that source has asked that we freely give to others what we have received. In the same verse, we're even told that our reward in heaven will be great if we do these things, and we will be sons of God. Wow! To love freely is an expression of sonship. Not only does it free those around us; it frees us from the burden of judging their worthiness to receive it, which is not a burden we were created to carry!

Prayer

God, I can't count the number of times You've offered Your free gift of love to me! Every time, I feel so deeply known and so truly loved. Holy Spirit, give me hints throughout the day about who I can offer free gifts of affection to! I know You'll partner with me as I choose to love them without expecting anything back. You gave me unconditional love, and I am so grateful for this gift. I now offer it freely to others, too.

Reflection

1. Choose someone you can love freely and liberally today through words and actions.

   _____

   _____

   _____

   _____

2. Observe how you feel before and after doing or saying something loving.

   _____

   _____

   _____

   _____

3. Observe if your love impacts their behavior, attitude, or words.

   _____

   _____

   _____

   _____

4. How might you change for the better if you no longer felt you had to spend time judging people's worthiness to receive your love?

   _____

   _____

   _____

   _____

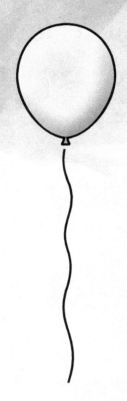

Day 32 – Openness

WORDS ARE
A WAY TO LOVE

"Kind words produce happiness. How often have we ourselves been made happy by kind words, in a manner and to an extent which we are unable to explain!"

Frederick William Faber

> *"Therefore encourage one another and build each other up, just as in fact you are doing."*
>
> 1 Thessalonians 5:11 ESV

The Bible says that "life and death are in the power of the tongue." The words we use are important to all of us. It's through our words we make positive and negative spiritual agreements. When we use our words negatively, gossip, complain, or curse each other, we're using our tongue to partner with death, but when we use our words positively, to encourage, celebrate, or bless each other, we're using our tongue to partner with life!

Is it words of affirmation that make you come alive and feel loved? Do you know people who thrive on encouragement? Thessalonians 5:11 says, "Therefore encourage each other and build each other up." This verse recognizes the power of our words to "put courage into" and strengthen each other. For people whose love language is words of affirmation, this is even more important. We can love them well by using positive words to communicate our love and appreciation to them. God cares so much about words! He provided us with His Word to comfort us, encourage us, and demonstrate His love for us. He sent Jesus, whom John referred to as "The Word made flesh."

For "words" people, receiving and giving love is about taking the time to articulate what we mean to each other. For them, someone may show love in a hundred ways, but if they've never said, "I love you," it won't get through to their heart. Trust is built with words, positive body language, and tone of voice. If you'll sit and talk something through, affirm, and encourage them, you'll build trust quickly. Similarly, careless negative words have a deeper impact on them than others. You can love "words" people well by leaving messages, writing cards, or remembering to tell them how you feel when you're with them. You'll find they'll often be doing the same for you! We can use words not only to show love to others, but to accept God's love for us! What promise over your life can you speak positively over? A great first step is to try a "negativity fast" for a day and see how, with intention, you can increase speaking positively over your life and the lives of those around you!

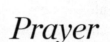

Prayer

God, thank You for speaking words of encouragement!
I love reading Your words, sensing Your voice, and receiving prayers.
Thank You for creating us to hear Your voice! Where my spouse, friends, or family are
"words of affirmation" people, I commit to taking the time to articulate what I feel
toward them, to offer them words of encouragement during tough times
and words of celebration when things are going well.
Thank You, Jesus, that my words encompass creative power!
I choose to create life with my words over my friends and family today.
I commit to showing them love through my words to encourage,
build up, and edify.

Reflection

1. How comfortable are you with giving and receiving love through words?

    _____

    _____

    _____

    _____

2. Are there any lies you've believed that make it harder for you to receive love through words?

    _____

    _____

    _____

    _____

3. What might you learn about "speaking" this love language from observing others?

    _____

    _____

    _____

    _____

4. On your calendar, write down a date and way you can practice showing love to someone through words of encouragement.

    _____

    _____

    _____

    _____

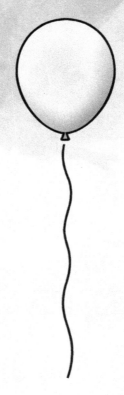

LIVING AS A VICTOR
NOT A VICTIM

*"The victim mindset dilutes the human potential.
By not accepting personal responsibility for our circumstances,
we greatly reduce our power to change them."*

Dr. Steve Maraboli

God is our rescuer! He is so good to give us examples of this aspect of His nature throughout scripture. One example is the story of Gideon. Gideon was full of fear and hiding in a winepress, but God came to the rescue. He not only physically protected Gideon from harm during battles; He emotionally protected him by reminding him he was not a victim, but a conqueror. He did not need to be full of fear, but full of valor. God reminded Gideon that he was an owner of his own process and God will do the same for you! God is invested in reminding you that He created you to steward your own life!

When I (Ally) was clinically depressed in my teens, I felt completely like a victim. The problem was, as a victim, I was handing over all my self-control and trying to make others control me by rescuing me. If they hurt me, I felt I was controlled by them as well. I later discovered that if I often felt like a victim, that meant I was unconsciously trying to control others into fulfilling the role of rescuer that God never designed them to fulfill. That was exactly what made me an easy target for people who wanted to victimize me. All they had to do was pretend to be a rescuer for ten minutes, and I was hooked. I constantly gave away my control to allow others to control how I felt. I constantly felt depleted and defeated. I eventually learned that thoughts related to feeling like a victim can become an unhealthy obsession and even have addictive qualities. It may feel "right," but it destroys your life. Thinking of myself as a victim and hoping someone else would rescue me was like a drug that dulled me into inaction and cemented me in victimhood. I had to take steps, with God's help, to imitate Him, and become my biggest resource to rescue myself. As I did, I felt the shackles come free, and felt like I was able to live again and determine my own fate.

A person with a victim mentality is stuck trying to figure out if each person is their perpetrator or their savior, instead of seeing people as people. Often, people who play the victim don't have friends, because healthy people do not like to be controlled into being a rescuer. This perpetuates the cycle of the victim feeling like more of a victim: attacked, abandoned, ignored, or unworthy. Empowered people set a standard for how they want to be treated, and how they want to treat others, free of this dynamic. Philippians 4:13 says, "I can do all things through Christ who strengthens me." God has already rescued you, and given you the power to feel rescued by taking control back for your own life and choices. We can all learn to be a conqueror, creating an environment in which everybody in our lives, including us, is free to be themselves.

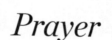

Prayer

God, thank You that in Your kingdom there are no victims, only overcomers!
Where I've mistaken myself for a victim in the past, I now declare myself a victor!
I joyfully take responsibility for my life, choices, and problems.
I no longer need a pity party, because who would pity a child of the King?
I no longer look to others to rescue me, because my savior lives within me.
I know You have given me everything I need to overcome in every situation,
and You are faithful! So, I look at life through Your eyes
of victory from this day on.

Reflection

1. Do you cast yourself or some people into the role of being either a victim, a rescuer, or a bad guy?

    _____

    _____

    _____

    _____

2. How might you be able to accept God as your rescuer in more areas of your life?

    _____

    _____

    _____

    _____

3. What are the actions and behaviors you think are associated with being an overcomer?

    _____

    _____

    _____

    _____

4. What thought(s) might you need to let go of and surrender to God in order to see yourself as an overcomer?

    _____

    _____

    _____

    _____

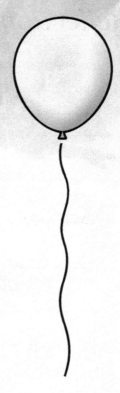

Day 34– Openness

QUALITY TIME
IS A WAY TO LOVE

"The friend that always finds time to spend with you without consulting his or her calendar is a true friend."

Ellen J. Barrier

"And do not forget to do good and to share with others, for with such sacrifices God is pleased."

Hebrews 13:16 NIV

Jesus was unhurried in His commitment to spending quality time with people. We see stories all over scripture of Jesus sitting and eating with His disciples, talking with them and teaching them. Likewise, He visits other people's houses, including those of tax collectors and sinners, reclines at their tables and spends time with them. He shows His interest in people by being willing to stay, eat, and talk. This is probably why He bonded with the most unlikely people—they were the ones He gave His time to, and who gave their time to Him. Can you imagine how loved the sinners must have felt, knowing Jesus not only came to forgive their sins but actually wanted to know them?

If we want solid relationship connections, we must learn to adjust and yield to new ways of giving and receiving love. One of these ways is through quality time. Do you feel loved and cherished when people spend time with you? Or maybe you know somebody who receives love primarily in this way. People who give and receive love like this feel connected when we find them interesting and prove it by hanging out with them. If we want to love these people well, we get to learn what they value so we can better reach them. This way our free acts of love can be received as love, and we can target our love in ways that will have the greatest impact. Hebrews tells us it pleases God when we sacrifice to do good for others, and this is one way we can love others well.

When a "quality time" person invites you into a conversation or to join them in an activity, this is a great opportunity for you to send the message: "I am interested in you!" When you take time out of your day, give them your full attention, and make space for them, they feel loved. The opposite is also true. You can buy the "quality time" person all the gifts in the world, but if you don't show up for them, it won't mean much. When you don't make time to engage with them, you send the message you're not interested in them, that they are not important to you or worst of all, that you don't love them. The good news is, quality time is not quantity time. It's not about how much time you spend, but the level of genuine interest and engagement you give. To be imitators of Christ, we are given the privilege of getting to share love with others and to share it in a way they can receive it. We can also benefit from this, as it allows our relational connection to continue to grow! See what happens when you engage in the activity or conversation with all of your energy and attention and engage with them on the deepest level!

Prayer

God, thank You for not being in a hurry. You always take the time to linger with me, to listen to everything I have to say, and to sit with me even when I have no words. Where my spouse, friends, or family are "quality time" people, I commit to loving them in this way. I choose to make space in my schedule, remove distractions, and be generous with my time to demonstrate my love for them, just as You always demonstrate Your love toward me! I know that You will abundantly bless the time we spend together and lead us into a deeper relationship with each other and You.

Reflection

1. What do you think are the most important ingredients that make up quality time?

    _____
    _____
    _____
    _____

2. Do you know anyone who is really good at showing love through quality time?

    _____
    _____
    _____
    _____

3. What have you observed about how others communicate love through quality time, and is it something you might try?

    _____
    _____
    _____
    _____

4. On your calendar, write down a date and a way you can practice showing love to someone by giving quality time.

    _____
    _____
    _____
    _____

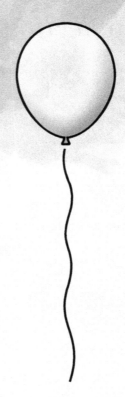

Day 35 – Ownership

REMOVING FEAR
IN CONVERSATION

"My fear doesn't stand a chance when I stand in your love."

Josh Baldwin

"'Do not be afraid of their faces, For I am with you to deliver you,' says the Lord."

Jeremiah 1:8 NKJV

God is good at displacing our fear with His truth, and often invites us to replace the fear in our heart with His love and strength. Consider Jeremiah. He was called as a youth to deliver God's word to groups of people who did not want to listen! Talk about some fear-inducing conversations. Jeremiah expressed his feeling that others would not listen to him. But God came in comforting Jeramiah, saying, "'Do not be afraid of them, for I am with you and will rescue you,' declares the LORD" (Jeremiah 1:8 NIV). This word no doubt carried Jeremiah through many difficult conversations! It likely kept him from prematurely abandoning his goals.

Most of us do not have to fear physical death from a conversation (as Jeramiah did), but we may still often fear our hearts being hurt, misunderstood, or ignored. When we're learning great communication skills, our goal should be to remove this fear from our conversations. Fear brings out the worst in us. When any of us get scared, we tend to react in primitive, even unhelpful, ways. If we can remove fear, we set the stage for meaningful communication and responses that line up with our priority of staying connected, expressing our needs, and meeting the needs of others. This includes the firm beliefs that we are worthy of God's love, worthy of our own healthy self-love, and able to share our love with others.

The first step to displacing our fear in our conversations is to identify when we start feeling fear in a conversation. Often, we will sense this first in our body. Our back or stomach will tighten; our jaw will clench. This is the time, if possible, when we need to take a pause within ourselves or with our conversation. We may need to take a break and come back to the conversation later. During this pause, ask yourself what you need and what is causing the fear. Most of the time, we're fearful of not getting our needs met or of being controlled. The good news is, in healthy relationships these fears can be easily resolved if we are brave enough to share them.

We must start to allow the voice of love to speak louder than the voice of fear in our own heart. Remember what God said to Jeraimiah: "I will rescue you." Another translation translates it as, "I will protect you." When we trust God to help us protect and, if need be, rescue our hearts, we no longer have to fear that we can receive God's love in all our conversations. We can be the voice of love to help reduce others' fear as well.

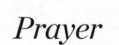

Prayer

*God, You are the source of love that casts out all fear.
I choose to bring You my fears today, knowing that You want to meet me
with the whisper of Your spirit. I refuse to tolerate fear in my life,
but continue to receive Your love that perfects my heart. As I grow in love,
may it overflow into my relationships and displace every fear. I desire to enter into
every relationship with You or with others to lead with love and not presume or
entertain fear. Thank You, God, for Your overwhelming love
that allows me to do this.*

Reflection

1. What is a phrase or two you might use to demonstrate you value another person's thoughts or feelings, even when you disagree?

    _____

    _____

    _____

    _____

2. What are the fears that commonly come up for you in conversations with others? Do you fear they will think poorly of you? Are you afraid they might take advantage of you or lie to you?

    _____

    _____

    _____

    _____

3. Take a moment to think about your fear. If your fear was true, what would that mean about you? Often our fears are tied to fears about ourselves, our worth, our lovability, or our sense of control.

    _____

    _____

    _____

    _____

4. Write a few lines of comfort to yourself about God's view of you.

    _____

    _____

    _____

    _____

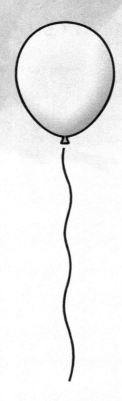

Day 36– Openness

SERVING IS
A WAY TO LOVE

"Let us never forget that authentic power is service,
which has its radiant culmination on the Cross."

Pope Francis

*"This is how we know what love is:
Jesus Christ laid down His life for us.
And we ought to lay down our lives for
our brothers and sisters."*

1 John 3:16 NIV

Servanthood is a key theme in the scriptures, as we see articulated beautifully in John 3:16. "This is how we know what love is: Jesus Christ laid down His life for all of us. And we ought to lay down our lives for our brothers and sisters." Jesus came as the servant of all, and also revealed to us that true greatness is to serve others.

In John 20, the mother of Zebedee's sons brings her sons to Jesus. She asks Jesus to let the brothers sit on each side of His throne in His kingdom. Jesus answers and says, "You do not know what you ask. Are you able to drink the cup I'm able to drink and be baptized with the baptism that I am baptized with?" They are looking for worldly greatness but don't understand the kingdom. Jesus explains, saying, "you know that the rulers of the Gentiles lord it over them, and those who are great exercise authority over them, yet it shall not be so among you. Whoever desires to be great among you, let him be your servant...just as the Son of Man did not come to be served, but to serve, and to give His life a ransom for many."

Some people give and receive love through acts of service. You can speak words all you like, but until they see the evidence of your love through actions, words feel like empty promises. "Acts of service" people feel most loved when you offer them intentional acts of kindness. If they arrive at work or at home, and can see that things have been done for them, they instantly feel loved. If, however, they see that nothing has been done, or you left them more to do, their stress rises and they don't feel loved. The key to loving an "acts of service" person well is to recognize that they are looking for you to do things for them before they ask it of you. If they have to ask, it negates the gesture altogether. If you are an "acts of service" person, it helps to communicate your needs clearly so that those around you have the best chance of meeting them. Once you figure them out, acts of service are easy to bless as small gestures often go a long way. "Acts of service" people naturally understand this and love to serve others with their actions. Their actions are intended to impact others for the greater good, and we can all learn the art of servanthood from them as we aspire to true kingdom greatness!

───────────── ✦ ─────────────

Prayer

God, thank You that Your son is the ultimate demonstration of servanthood. He is my model for how to live my life. There is such joy in imitating Him and serving Your people, Lord! Provide me with plenty of opportunities to do this! You value humility; therefore, I value humility. You see my heart to serve You and others and are so pleased with me! As I grow in servanthood, I know You increase the joy in my heart, and enable me to be a cheerful giver!

Reflection

1. How comfortable are you with giving and receiving love through acts of service?

    _____

    _____

    _____

    _____

2. Do you know anyone who is really good at loving through acts of service?

    _____

    _____

    _____

    _____

3. What might you learn about "speaking" this love language from observing others who are good at showing love through acts of service?

    _____

    _____

    _____

    _____

4. On your calendar, write down a date and way you can practice showing love to someone through an act of service.

    _____

    _____

    _____

    _____

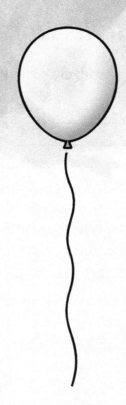

Day 37 – Ownership

BUILDING INTIMACY WITH OTHERS

"Love is like breathing. You take it in and let it out."

Wally Lamb

*"Lord, you have searched me and known me. You know my
sitting down and my rising up. You understand my thoughts
afar off. You comprehend my path and my lying down,
And are acquainted with all my ways."*

Psalm 139:1-3 NKJV

Relational intimacy is not just an experience for the fortunate; it is available to all of us. The experience of intimacy comes when we feel we're fully known and loved for who we are, and when we know and love someone else in return. This complete acceptance brings fulfillment and satisfaction to us. One of God's greatest desires is for us to have an intimate relationship with Him. Psalm 139:1-3 says, "Lord, you have searched me and known me. You know my sitting down and my rising up. You understand my thoughts afar off. You comprehend my path and my lying down, and are acquainted with all my ways." This is the foundation for all other intimacy.

A safe place for intimacy is created when two people can consistently complete the "trust cycle." The trust cycle looks like this: a need is expressed, a need is understood, and a need is met. The first step of the trust cycle is to be willing to be vulnerable. The more trust cycles we complete, the easier this is to do. Over time we build enough trust that we can clearly say, "We can be ourselves together because you can see into me and I can see into you." The first place we practice this trust cycle is with God. Intimacy with God is created in prayer, by sharing our heart with Him, honestly expressing needs and allowing Him to meet us in them. If we've successfully built intimacy with God, building intimacy with others is easier because we already feel fully loved and accepted.

Intimacy doesn't happen overnight. It starts small, and as we increase vulnerability it begins to grow progressively. In 1 Samuel 18, Jonathan and David make a covenant of friendship to each other, but this bond grows stronger as they complete trust cycles with each other. Jonathan challenges his own father to protect David from being put to death. Their friendship is not just an announcement of intimacy; it's proven time and time again in consistently building trust with each other. This is a process that David first practiced with God, where he shared his heart with God, and saw God protect him from Goliath and wild animals. In the same way, God wants to lead you into intimate relationships, but it often starts by allowing yourself to be intimate and honest with Him.

Prayer

God, thank You that I thrive in intimate relationships. Just as You've taught me intimacy in my relationship with you, I choose to build intimacy in my relationships with others. Thank You for creating me to love and be loved! Areas in my life that I am not thriving in I can change with Your help. I can build a better, more intimate network of relationships. Teach me like You taught Noah to build according to your pattern and plan. I want to build relationships with Your help, Jesus. Thank You for assisting me.

Reflection

1. What does intimacy with God look like in your life (when, why, and how do you feel intimate with Him)?

   _____
   _____
   _____
   _____

2. What would you like to experience in a relationship that you are not yet experiencing?

   _____
   _____
   _____
   _____

3. Brainstorm ways to communicate your need in an open, lighthearted, non-demanding, and non-shaming way.

   _____
   _____
   _____
   _____

4. How can you grow toward not just meeting a need once, but meeting it consistently for a person who shares a need with you?

   _____
   _____
   _____
   _____

Day 38– Openness

BEING OPEN
TO RESTORATION

*"A person who has been punished is not less inclined to behave
in a given way; at best, he learns how to avoid punishment."*

Dr. Burrhus Frederick Skinner

*"As far as the east is from the west,
So far has He removed our transgressions from us."*

Psalm 103:12 NKJV

The glorious truth of the gospel is that Jesus took our punishment upon himself! Punishment might be normal in our society, but as covenant sons and daughters in the kingdom, we get to live from a different paradigm. If we want to learn how to eliminate punishment from our relationships, our first step must be to stop punishing ourselves and receive the fullness of grace that Jesus purchased for us. Psalm 103:12 tells us, "As far as the east is from the west, so far has He removed our transgressions from us." If God has removed it, who are we to try to keep finding it and apply it? Punishment threatens our connection with God, ourselves, and others.

Joseph is a great example of this. His brothers left him in a pit, sold him into a life of slavery, separated him from his family and everything he ever knew, and caused grief to his father who loved him. And yet, when Joseph meets his brothers again years later, he doesn't punish them. They have already experienced the consequences of their actions in their life, and the sadness and distress their choices brought on their father. Joseph does not allow their actions to dictate his decision to trust God or restore his relationship with them. He embraces them, blesses them, and shares with them the success he has found. Joseph recognizes that God was in control of his life all along, and welcomes the restoration of his relationship with his brothers. He allows them to show him that they are changed, and then invites them back into a full relationship.

Everybody makes mistakes, and punishment usually comes up when we either make a mistake ourselves and fall into patterns of self-punishment, or when somebody else makes a mistake and our default is to punish

166

them for it. We need to have a fear-free, control-free plan for dealing with mistakes. This looks like staying engaged and curious, setting boundaries, and walking through a process of restoration. An owner of their self-process says, "I will be okay no matter what you do and I will never stop loving you!" Punishment is a heavy burden that keeps us from living a life of freedom and keeps us from being open to embracing people as they are, and keeps us from brainstorming possible solutions. It keeps us in a victim mentality, which keeps us from making proactive choices. If we want to be open to God's plan and restoration in our lives, we must start by not punishing ourselves or others!

Prayer

God, thank You that in You I am free from punishment!
Where I've used relational distance as punishment in the past,
I step into Your new standard today. Where I've experienced this from others,
I see now that their actions were probably rooted in fear or pain
and release forgiveness to them. I am in awe of what You bought for me on the cross:
endless grace and total forgiveness! Punishment never has to be part of my love again.
Instead, I'm so grateful that You have a plan for restoration for every situation.
I choose Your plan today and receive Your grace!

Reflection

1. Are there mistakes or shortcomings you continue to punish yourself for? (Punishment may look like using negative, derogatory, or unkind language, using shame or anger to try to exert control, refusing to take care of yourself or someone else because you feel it is not deserved, etc.)

   _____

   _____

   _____

   _____

2. Come up with a short phrase or prayer you can use to help remind yourself that you are now free from punishment.

   _____

   _____

   _____

   _____

3. Are there mistakes or shortcomings you continue to punish others for?

   _____

   _____

   _____

   _____

4. What would you need to change in order to emulate Christ by offering forgiveness instead of punishment?

   _____

   _____

   _____

   _____

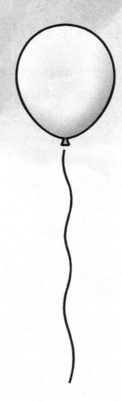

Day 39– Ownership

MEETING NEEDS
WITH HEALING WORDS

"As soon as healing takes place, go out and heal somebody else."

Maya Angelou

"The words of the reckless pierce like swords,
but the tongue of the wise brings healing."

Relational health rests on good communication. Some people seem as if they are born able to intuitively communicate well, diffuse tension, and formulate good responses in the heat of the moment, but for most of us, good communication is a skill that we can and must learn. Proverbs 12:18 says, "The words of the reckless pierce like swords, but the tongue of the wise brings healing." We've all experienced the sharp cut of reckless words (maybe most often from ourselves), and most likely had moments where we've hurt others with our words. When we are intentional to think of words that will heal in our relationships, we will find ourselves benefiting from being in a relationship where we reap the rewards of being around healed and healthier people. When we offer ourselves words of healing instead of reckless words, we are able to more fully embrace God's healing and life for us as well. This, indeed, is wisdom!

As we try to understand what kind of words heal, it helps to ask ourselves, "What does that person need?" When we take the time to figure out what that person needs in order to feel loved, our "I love you" messages are more likely to hit their target. The easiest way to know is just to ask! Then we can move toward actually resolving needs with solutions. We also need to ask ourselves this question and share that information in a kind, truthful, and loving way. When we express our true thoughts and needs in a loving way, we open the door to be loved and to love others for who we truly are. This can mean giving of ourselves by sharing our feelings and desires, or what we specifically love about that person. It can also mean not getting so caught up in a hard moment that we lose the big picture of who they are and cut them down to someone lesser than they are. Intentional words communicated in love strengthen the bonds of connection and allow us to bring healing to each other.

How does God deal with us when we express unhappiness or our needs to Him? Does He shame us and bring up our faults? Or, does He cover them in love? In 1 Samuel, Hannah desperately wants a son. She can't eat; she's weeping constantly. She's comparing herself to her rival, who is provoking her and making her feel worse. Many of us would have advised her to just accept her lot, but Hannah expresses her need to God. When Eli the priest sees her weeping, she explains that she is pouring out her soul to the Lord. Eli blesses her and offers healing words instead of judgmental or condemning words. He says, "Go in peace, and may the God of Israel give you what you've asked for." The Bible tells us that "she was no longer downcast," which tells me that God met her need in that moment, as well as later when she became pregnant. Hannah valued her need enough to express it, and God, through Eli, met her there and blessed her with healing.

Prayer

God, thank You that You value me more than I can imagine,
and deeply care about my needs! As I pay attention to my life, I choose to grow
in awareness of how I respond to my own needs and those of others.
As I practice great communication skills, show me the heart of others.
Guide my thoughts and tongue toward healing and life, instead of destruction and death.
Enlighten my heart and mind to speak forth the words of life just like Jesus.
Thank You, God, that You are the best communicator.

Reflection

1. Identify some people you are close to, and take the time to consider (even ask them) what they need to feel loved.

    _____

    _____

    _____

    _____

2. Identify needs, desires, or preferences you feel are hard to express.

    _____

    _____

    _____

    _____

3. Have you expressed these needs to God honestly?

    _____

    _____

    _____

    _____

4. How or when might you practice expressing your needs in low-stake situations when emotions are at peace?

    _____

    _____

    _____

    _____

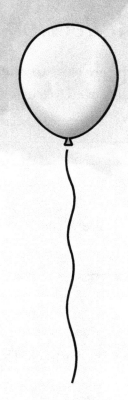

Day 40 – Openness

WHAT'S GOING ON
IN YOUR HEART?

*"Communication leads to community, that is,
to understanding, intimacy, and mutual valuing."*

Dr. Rollo May

I n the book of Nehemiah, we learn that Nehemiah was deeply saddened to learn that the walls of Jerusalem were destroyed. He says, "When I heard these things, I sat down and wept. For some days I mourned..." (Nehemiah 1:4 NIV). He then goes back to his work as cupbearer for the king, and the king notices his sadness. This must have been an intimidating situation to be truthful in. Nehemiah was a servant in the king's household, if a highly honored one, and may have assumed his personal needs, feelings, and desires weren't important to the king. But when the king asks, Nehemiah freely shares his heart with him. In response, the king offers to meet his need, saying, "What is it you want?" And then he grants him all he asks and more.

A great first step in learning to communicate well is to pay attention to our thoughts, feelings, and needs and to respect their value. Then we can start doing the same for others! We must always check ourselves when we're tempted to invalidate someone's experiences or heart. We also must not take it personally or feel that it means we hurt them intentionally. If we can get good at understanding what is going on inside and pick up our early indicators of unease, we'll find it much easier to communicate clearly to others. We can have regular "tune-ups" instead of massive breakdowns. Jesus said, "Out of the abundance of the heart his mouth speaks" (Matthew 12:34 NKJV). Great communication happens when we value what's going on in our hearts and take the time to find out what we need instead of reacting to a situation or conversation.

174

If our hearts (our internal reality) are governed by fear, then we'll communicate fear through our words, body language, and facial expressions. If our hearts are governed by faith, hope, and love, we will communicate this reality instead. We already know that fear is never helpful in building relational connection. If fear is governing our hearts, much of our communication will be pointed toward the goal of hiding what's inside. We may pretend to be happy when we're actually heartbroken, or pretend something that's hurt us doesn't matter. We do this because we're afraid of being honest and being hurt even more, but this only erodes trust and prevents connection. Instead, if we value our heart, find out what it needs, and take ownership to share it, we will build trust and connection. This is the only route to true, lasting relationships.

Prayer

God, You know my heart better than anyone.
You know where it has been hurt and where it has been cherished.
Where rejection, frustration, and fear have been part of my past, thank You that I don't need to partner with them in my future. My heart culture is one that carries the abundance of Your love. Search my heart and know me. Remove anything in my heart that keeps me from loving You and those You have given me. Thank You, God, for Your wonderful Holy Spirit. Send Your love to wash my heart every day.

Reflection

1. How often do you find yourself struggling to communicate when you feel sad, hurt, or misunderstood?

   _____

   _____

   _____

   _____

2. Do you think others struggle to communicate these feelings to you?

   _____

   _____

   _____

   _____

3. How do you first start to recognize you feel uneasy in a conversation (does your body feel tense, do you start to look away, do you start apologizing unnecessarily)?

   _____

   _____

   _____

   _____

4. How might you change these behaviors that demonstrate unease and demonstrate confidence in yourself instead?

   _____

   _____

   _____

   _____

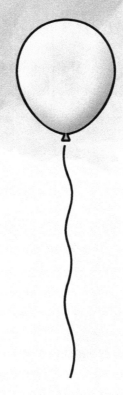

Day 41 – Ownership

TAKING TIME FOR YOURSELF

*"It's okay to take time for yourself. We give so much of ourselves
to others, and we need to be fueled both physically and mentally.
If we are in balance, it helps us in all our interactions."*

Faith Hill

"So He Himself often withdrew into the wilderness and prayed."

Luke 5:16 NKJV

Jesus had no problem asking for what He needed. He valued His needs and was able to express them. We see this in how He frequently set time aside to pray and be alone. How often do you set aside time to be alone, get in touch with your heart, and identify your needs? In the midst of our busy lives, it can be easy to put everyone else's needs above our own. Though it may feel counter-intuitive, prioritizing "you" actually gives you the information you need about yourself to share your needs in ways that will resolve problems before they start. It also fuels you so you can meet the needs of others in a healthy way. Luke 5:16 says, "So He Himself often withdrew into the wilderness and prayed." It does not say, "Then Jesus felt guilty because He felt He should have spent every moment with His family or He should have healed more people." No! Taking care of His needs was what gave Him strength to continue to walk in His calling!

Taking time to be alone and become aware of our thoughts, feelings, and needs shows that we value what's going on in our hearts. When we value what's going on for us, our relationship with our heart changes. This helps us be the best communicator we can by affirming our value, and allowing others to do the same. Prioritizing yourself may look like seeking healing from past experiences that lead you to fear the truth of your heart and how it may be received. This gives you time to identify patterns of communication that are helpful and which are not. It sets the course for positive change. Valuing your heart is the only way to start to really know how to value another person's heart.

In Jesus's Parable of the Sower, He says, "The seed on good soil stands for those who hear the word, retain it, and by persevering, produce a crop" (Luke 8:15). Jesus demonstrated a lifestyle of fruitfulness by seeking God's word in prayer, taking time to meditate on it, and persevering until He saw the fruit. Following His times of prayer were always times of great miracles. In the same way, taking time to find God's wisdom for our relationships, identifying our needs, and learning to communicate them requires perseverance, but will also produce great fruit. Start today by setting aside some time to pray and connect with your heart.

Prayer

God, thank You for prioritizing me.
Thank You for teaching me how to protect my closest relationships.
I commit to setting boundaries on my time to protect the priorities of my heart.
I know that I can't be everything to everyone,
and I choose today to make decisions about my time.
Show me what You would do with the time that I have.
How would You prioritize yourself today, Jesus?
Show me what self-care is from Your perspective.
I look to You because You are where my help comes from.
You are my guide and my shepherd.

Reflection

1. Do you often feel guilt for taking time to yourself, or pressure to help others instead?

   _____

   _____

   _____

   _____

2. Write out five to ten of your top priorities in life.

   _____

   _____

   _____

   _____

3. When people make demands of your time, do you find it easy to say "yes" or "no" in line with your priorities?

   _____

   _____

   _____

   _____

4. What small change can you make this week to prioritize yourself?

   _____

   _____

   _____

   _____

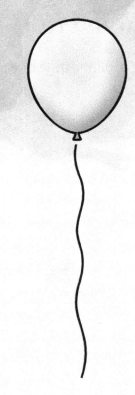

Day 42– Openness

BEING GENUINE BUILDS INTIMACY

"Be your authentic self. Your authentic self is who you are when you have no fear of judgment...your fictional self is who you are when you have a social mask on to please everyone else."

Dr. Phil

"I sought the Lord, and He heard me, And delivered me from all my fears. They looked to Him and were radiant, And their faces were not ashamed."

Psalm 34:4-5 NKJV

In her groundbreaking TED talk, "The Power of Vulnerability," Dr. Brene Brown shares deep insight from her research on human connection. Shame is what invites us to hide our feelings. It's the fear that we're "not enough" and won't be loved if we're truly known. But, according to Brene, the opposite of shame is "wholeheartedness." To be wholehearted is to decide to show up, show yourself as you are, and choose to live with the deep conviction that you are enough.

When we first get to know a new person, our conversations start off surface-level and light, often involving easy subjects like the weather, the news or brief exchanges like, "How are you?" and, "Oh, we're fine." These conversations are comfortable, safe, and appropriate for when we first meet someone. They require very little from us. However, as we get to know people better, our conversations must increase toward more deep and genuine exchanges. Many people avoid being genuine about their thoughts and needs out of a fear of being hurt. This will never build strong relationships.

Some confuse being genuine with being vulnerable. We all should be very careful to not be vulnerable with people who have not passed "tests" of intimacy that demonstrate they are capable of handling our heart wisely. We further would say, it is our job to make ourselves strong in the Lord to where we lose fear of shame. Brene Brown would say vulnerability is the act of showing another person yourself, unashamed and honest. But if we are secure in ourselves and Christ, we should be growing toward a life where shame has no hold and we are more honest about who we

182

really are. The best of human relationships happens when we see, know, and love each other. Psalm 34:4-5 says, "I sought the Lord and He heard me, And delivered me from all my fears. They looked to Him and were radiant, And their faces were not ashamed." We are already accepted, loved, and treasured by the Lord, and He has delivered us from all our shame. This is where we can draw strength from as we seek to be more genuine with others.

✦

Prayer

God, thank You for meeting me exactly where I'm at.
Just as You value being genuine in my relationship with You,
I value being genuine in my relationships with others.
I choose to let down my masks so that I can be seen,
and to encourage others to do the same.
Show me how to be transparent in my exchanges
and show me how to let people in.
I want to open up my heart and life to be known by You and others.
Send Your comfort to my weak and vulnerable areas and give me strength
to be fully known and fully loved.
Thank You, Jesus.

Reflection

1. Write a few lines about what first comes to mind when you think
    of the word "vulnerability."

    _____

    _____

    _____

    _____

2. Now, imagine looking from God's perspective. Do you think
    He believes the same thing you do about vulnerability?

    _____

    _____

    _____

    _____

3. How often do you think Jesus made himself vulnerable or
    felt vulnerable?

    _____

    _____

    _____

    _____

4. What tools do you see Him use to overcome this?
    (Prayer, alone time, faith, communicating fears, etc.)

    _____

    _____

    _____

    _____

Day 43– Ownership

SHARING OUR PEACE

"Peace is not the absence of something; it's the presence of someone."

Bill Johnson

"Peace I leave with you, My peace I give to you; not as the world gives do I give to you. Let not your heart be troubled, neither let it be afraid."

John 14:27 NKJV

To move toward successful communication, we must have some skills that we can use to not just manage our own stress in a conversation, but to lower the stress of those we're communicating with. When others are anxious, we are likely not going to understand the full picture and conversations will not be as effective, as they are communicating out of fear. One way to help lower fear is by steadfastly communicating love and acceptance of the person, even when we do not like their behavior. When we separate the person from the behavior, we're able to offer unconditional love and acceptance, and therefore lower fear in every conversation. We reassure them that we value their desires, feelings, and needs with our words, body language, and facial expressions.

Like most relational processes, this is a process we must learn to enact with ourselves first. If we come into a conversation thinking we may lose the relationship if we share how we really feel, sharing becomes a really big deal. We are sharing thoughts from the unrenewed mind. Thoughts from the mind of flesh, which fears we are not loved and fully accepted by God. We sow peace when we focus on sharing that we are committed to the goal of understanding and resolution. We first can identify fear in tone, body language, and expressions. These can clue us in to help us shift our focus to reassurance and peace before continuing the conversation. When either of us notices a tone of stress or frustration, we take that as a cue to say, "We're on the same team here. How can we work together to make things better?" This works like a vacuum to clean up any stress out of a communication problem.

In John 14:27, Jesus says, "Peace I leave with you, My peace I give to you; not as the world gives do I give to you." There is a supernatural peace available to us from God that we can cultivate within us and bring into our conversations. This doesn't mean that we accept every behavior, or that there aren't consequences for people's actions. What it does mean is that the relationship itself is not on the line and we extend the opportunity to work as a team.

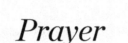

Prayer

God, thank You that I get to live in Your perfect peace.
Thank You that every display of love, no matter how small, is meaningful.
Thank You, God, that I cultivate an atmosphere of peace with my love, everywhere I go.
I lean on Your chest, Jesus, just as John the Beloved did, and I rest in Your arms.
Let Your heartbeat that I listen to lower my fear.
I know everything will work out because I am following You.
You are my prize. You are my reward.

Reflection

1. Who are the people you converse with on a daily and weekly basis?

   _____

   _____

   _____

   _____

2. With whom do you feel the most stress? Who might feel stressed talking to you?

   _____

   _____

   _____

   _____

3. How might you communicate to others that you're committed to the goal of understanding each other, instead of the goal of punishing behavior you do not like?

   _____

   _____

   _____

   _____

4. How might you work toward love instead of punishment (silent treatment, anger, accusations) when others do not perfectly meet your needs?

   _____

   _____

   _____

   _____

GIVING AND RECEIVING COMFORT

*"God does not comfort us to make us comfortable,
but to make us comforters."*

John Henry Jowett

"Blessed be the God and Father of our Lord Jesus Christ, the Father of mercies and God of all comfort, who comforts us in all our affliction, that we may be able to comfort those who are in any affliction, with the comfort with which we ourselves are comforted by God."

2 Corinthians 1:3-4 ESV

When we know how to receive comfort from the Holy Spirit, we're also able to give and receive comfort in our relationships in a healthy way. Do you know that God has promised to be our source of comfort? The Holy Spirit is called our comforter, and 2 Corinthians 1:3-4 reminds us that He is the "God of all comfort, who comforts us in all our affliction, that we may be able to comfort those who are in any affliction, with the comfort with which we ourselves are comforted by God." God has promised to be with us no matter what, and to comfort us in our times of needs. As we learn to turn to Him for our comfort instead of earthly things, we become a source of comfort for others, too.

When we're in pain, our natural instinct is to look for comfort. Unfortunately, this can look like pain-avoidance strategies rather than solution-focused ones. Pain-avoidance strategies can be anything that prevents us from actually solving the discomfort. This could be comfort eating, retail therapy, or more potentially destructive habits like attempting to control others, or doing drugs. It can be anything we look to instead of God to numb or escape our pain instead of thanking Him because pain helps alert us that we want and need something to change. We can also be tempted to try to control others into bringing pleasure and comfort to us, too. Allowing pain-avoidance strategies and control to become driving forces in our lives only leads to destruction. God asks us to partner with Him instead, the spirit of love. He is our ultimate source of love and comfort, and He leads us into healthy relationships with others where we take responsibility for ourselves and all others to do the same.

190

In John 14, we see Jesus comfort His disciples as they prepare for Him to leave. They are devastated that Jesus will be going, but Jesus reassures them that He is going ahead to prepare a place for them. He then tells them the Father will give them another advocate, the Holy Spirit, who will be with them always. Jesus tells them not to be troubled or afraid because the Holy Spirit will be with them, a source of supernatural peace. This same Holy Spirit is available to us and promises to be close to us in our greatest times of need. When we are connected to Him and His comfort, we can soothe relational fears and challenges effectively and move toward being owners in our relationships.

Prayer

God, thank You for Your Spirit that is the comforter.
Thank you for wanting me to experience comfort in my relationships with others.
Thank You, Jesus, that as I express my needs clearly and honestly, others have the opportunity to respond with comfort, just as I can offer this to others.
You bring me the comfort and love that I need to get through my day and succeed tomorrow. I desire to give and receive everything that you have for me, especially comfort. Teach me, Jesus, how to be a conduit of your love and comfort.

Reflection

1. How and when do you typically receive comfort from God?

   _____

   _____

   _____

   _____

2. Are there thoughts or feelings that make you upset or uncomfortable that you are trying to avoid, instead of accepting them and allowing God to transform them to feelings of comfort?

   _____

   _____

   _____

   _____

3. Are there areas in your life that you do not trust or depend on God to comfort you?

   _____

   _____

   _____

   _____

4. If so, what do you think is getting in the way of you pursuing Him as your comfort?

   _____

   _____

   _____

   _____

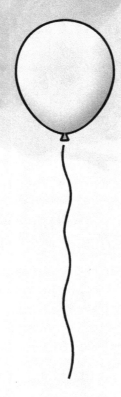

Day 45~ Ownership

WHAT ARE
YOU SOWING?

"As practice makes perfect, I cannot but make progress;
each drawing one makes, each study one paints, is a step forward"

Vincent Van Gogh

193

*"And let us not grow weary while doing good,
for in due season we shall reap if we do not lose heart."*

Galatians 6:9 NKJV

reat communication skills always take practice! It's especially important to practice the skills of healthy confrontation. I call it "brave communication strength training." As we practice and train ourselves to communicate clearly, we also build up a store of positive experiences that start to remove fear as we see the huge relational benefits to becoming a great communicator. Galatians 6:9 says, "And let us not grow weary while doing good, for in due season we shall reap if we do not lose heart." The biblical principle of sowing and reaping tells us that if we continue to practice good habits, we will see positive results in our lives.

Great relationships don't just happen; they're built over time through our choices to fine tune things instead of waiting for catastrophe. When you take ownership of a car, you perform regular maintenance on it, even if it is not convenient. The alternative to oil changes is a much bigger and more expensive problem! Taking ownership in relationships is much the same. When we practice sowing grace and love, it will improve in time. The exciting thing is as we improve what we sow, we reap something that is also improved. Alternatively, if we practice sowing negativity, anger, and self-righteousness, that is all we will have to reap.

We also need to be mindful we do not avoid our crop, when we see little pests or weeds creeping in. These are the weeds that can ruin all the good we are sowing. If we "let something go" that should have been communicated, we're missing an opportunity to connect to each other. It's amazing how quickly two people can drift apart if they're not fine-tuning things. We once heard an interview with Jordan B. Peterson and, in essence, he said it is much better to have many minor fights and arguments than one major betrayal. Discussing and resolving small frustrations and problems keeps your crop healthy; it keeps you connected and knowing the truth about where the other person stands. This, too, is something that many grow weary in, but the scripture reminds us that if we keep at it, we will reap if we do not lose heart.

Prayer

God, thank You for giving us a process in life where we can practice and improve. Thank You that You're faithful to provide everything I need to grow and develop new skills. Thank You that as I practice these skills, I'm forming new habits that will lead to happier, healthier relationships.
I choose to celebrate my progress today by following Your lead.
I will get up each and every day and practice love, practice communication, and practice healthy boundaries to become the best version of myself.
Thank You for helping me.
I love You, Jesus.

Reflection

1. Where do you most want to see a breakthrough in your relationships?

   _____

   _____

   _____

   _____

2. What tools and strategies could help you to partner with God for your breakthrough?

   _____

   _____

   _____

   _____

3. How do you tend to talk to yourself when you make mistakes or fall back into old patterns?

   _____

   _____

   _____

   _____

4. What can you celebrate about how far you've come?

   _____

   _____

   _____

   _____

Day 46– Openness

EQUAL VALUE

"What did Jesus know that enabled Him to do what He did?
Here's part of the answer: He knew the value of people.
He knew that each human being is a treasure. And because He did,
people were not a source of stress, but a source of joy."

Max Lucado

"Are not two sparrows sold for a penny? Yet not one of them will fall to the ground outside your Father's care. And even the very hairs of your head are all numbered. So don't be afraid; you are worth more than many sparrows."

Matthew 10:29-31 NIV

Every person is made in God's image, and is worthy of unconditional love. Jesus constantly made decisions that demonstrated His value for each person and His values of loving and respecting each person. He valued them, even when their culture or family did not. In Matthew 10:42, He illustrates this by telling the twelve, "And if anyone gives even a cup of cold water to one of these little ones who is my disciple, truly I tell you, that person will certainly not lose their reward." He treated everybody with honor and respect, which created space for them to be themselves and be empowered to be the best version of themselves. From tax collectors and sinners and even the Pharisees.

Values lead to behavior. Your values come out in everything you do. Part of being an owner of our own process is to live according to our chosen set of values. You can't choose values for others without operating in unhealthy control. Even Jesus did not require others to hold His values. He did not abandon or try to control Peter when Peter betrayed Him: He kept to his value system. By doing so, He created a way for Peter to realign with His own values. You can always choose to treat people and to respond to them according to your values. In Matthew 10:29-31, Jesus affirms our value by saying "Are not two sparrows sold for a penny? Yet not one of them will fall to the ground outside your Father's care. And even the very hairs of your head are all numbered. So don't be afraid; you are worth more than many sparrows." We know we are communicating well when we hold value for ourselves, and also value others. We can anchor our values in the teachings of Jesus because we know that in His goodness, He only commands what is best for us.

It is easy to look at Jesus and see what He valued; what He put His time and energy toward. What about you? What are those things you put your time and energy toward? If it is gossip or frustration with others, it will be hard to have conversations that communicate value. If it is self-interest, it will be hard to have conversations where others feel heard and enjoy communicating with you. When we understand how valuable every person is, we approach conversations with this in mind and demonstrate it with our actions. When we value healthy communication, we demonstrate our belief that the other person truly matters. When we value healthy communication, we communicate our feelings honestly and clearly. We demonstrate that every person in the conversation matters, and their feelings, desires, and needs matter too. Assertive communicators refuse to have relationships or conversations where both people do not have high, equal value. They work hard to protect the core values of honor and mutual respect.

Prayer

God, I choose to align my life to Your value system.
Thank You for Your word that teaches us about what really matters to You.
I choose to walk in Your ways and make Your priorities my priorities.
You value love, so I value love. You value people, so I value people.
Show me how to become a student of the word and follow closely
to Your thoughts and values. I want to be a reflection of who You are
inside and out. Guide my set of values so I can display You each and every day.
Thank You, Jesus, for empowering me to see You for who You are.

Reflection

1. What do you spend most of your time doing or thinking about (what do you value)?

   _____

   _____

   _____

   _____

2. Do the things you would say you value and what you actually put your time toward match, or are they different?

   _____

   _____

   _____

   _____

3. What would be different about your day tomorrow if you woke up and automatically valued yourself and others as much as God did?

   _____

   _____

   _____

   _____

4. What behaviors might you need to change so that others would see through your actions that you have a high equal value for yourself and others?

   _____

   _____

   _____

   _____

Day 47 – Ownership

RELATIONSHIPS
ARE TEAM SPORTS

"You do have choices.
No one is responsible for you and your life but you."

Geri Scazzero

"But let each one examine his own work, and then he will have rejoicing in himself alone, and not in another. For each one shall bear his own load."

Galatians 6:4-5 NKJV

When conflict occurs, it is tempting to try to control or convince others, but all of us are responsible for our own choices. It is each of our responsibility to manage the choices we're making regardless of what anyone else does. When we do this, we become powerful decision-makers in our relationships instead of victims of other people's choices.

In Luke 22, the Bible tells us about a dispute that rose up amongst the disciples. In this dispute, the disciples began to argue about who was the greatest. In essence saying, "I am right, good, and best; you are wrong, bad, and less than." Something interesting happens next. Jesus settles the dispute not by saying who is right and who is wrong, who did bad or good. He ignores that conversation and value system, as He knows it will not be helpful. Instead, He creates a different value system. He says, "Those who are the greatest among you should take the lowest rank, and the leader should be like a servant. " (NLT). This is an incredible reminder to stop trying to judge the other person's behavior as bad or worse than ours, as that conversation is never helpful. Any time we think we are doing better, we should be serving and helping the other person all the more.

Relationships are a team sport. If you play your best game, but score against your own teammates, you still will lose. Ally always encourages people to focus on what is "helpful" to the team instead of who is "right." You can be right, and extraordinarily unhelpful. You can be "wrong" but still take the next step to do what is helpful for the team. To use the word "helpful" means both can contribute and take responsibility for the team's outcome. Galatians 6:4-5 says, "But let each one examine his own work, and then he will have rejoicing in himself alone, and not in another. For each one shall bear his own load." This reminds us that each of us is responsible to manage our lives and take ownership of the choices we make. Just like when looking after your body, your goal should be to be responsible and do what you can do to prevent disease. However, even if you do get sick, you can be responsible and do things that make it better, or you can do things to make it worse!

Prayer

God, thank You that Your word demonstrates Your pleasure in seeing your children make good choices and steward their lives according to Your pattern. I joyfully choose to take full responsibility for my life today. Each choice that You made, Jesus, You owned that choice fully. Teach me to have the same level of ownership. I want to see down the road of my life's choices and own each one fully with Your vision, love, and direction. Show me the way and assist me in choosing the best life. Thank You, Jesus.

Reflection

1. When upset, do you spend more time focusing on what you do and say, or on what others do and say?

   _____

   _____

   _____

   _____

2. Do you tend to let yourself off the hook for disrespectful behavior by telling yourself it was someone else's fault you reacted that way?

   _____

   _____

   _____

   _____

3. Describe a situation that happened where you reacted when things did not go your way.

   _____

   _____

   _____

   _____

4. What could you change so that next time something similar happens, you move toward more assertiveness and self-control?

   _____

   _____

   _____

   _____

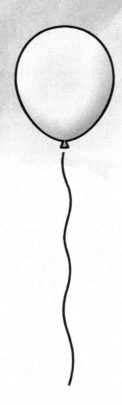

Day 48~ Openness

LIVING IN PURSUIT OF LOVE

"God knows our situation; He will not judge us as if we had no difficulties to overcome. What matters is the sincerity and perseverance of our will to overcome them."

C.S. Lewis

"I press on toward the goal to win the prize for which God has called me heavenward in Christ Jesus."

Phillippians 3:14 NIV

Part of imitating Jesus is the opportunity to love people first, to pursue their hearts, to seek to know them, think the best of them, and love them into the relationship God would want for you to have. When we pursue the hearts of others, we're taking ownership to offer unconditional love. Jesus actively pursues our hearts. 1 John 4:19 tells us, "We love Him because He first loved us." We walk in intimacy with Him when we pursue His heart as He pursues ours: "You will seek me and find me when you seek me with all of your heart" (Jer 29:13).

Some kinds of pursuit may feel easier to us than others. Perhaps if you've just met the man or woman of your dreams, pursuit feels like a joy rather than a burden. It might fill you with excitement and anticipation offering free gifts of love, finding out their love language, and planning ways to make them feel special. Then, there is the kind of pursuit that's harder, but even more crucial to do. It's the pursuit that's required to keep moving toward another person when they've hurt, disappointed, or betrayed you. This is when it really counts. It might be tempting to fall into fear-based reactions to run, hide, or freeze, but choosing to pursue them in this moment is the vulnerable act required to mend what's broken and strengthen connection.

When I think of pursuit, I can't help but think of the extraordinary story of Hosea. In Hosea's tragic story, God illustrates His never-ending love for His people, and His commitment to pursue them regardless of their behavior, until their relationship with Him is fully restored. Talk about unconditional love! We are part of this story, as God reconciled us to

206

Himself through the death and resurrection of Jesus. We now live in His perfect love, and get to extend that love to others. Jesus said, "Greater love has no one than this, than to lay down his life for his friends" (John 15:13). We can begin to pursue people well by laying down our fear, our need to be right, and our pain, and continuing to move toward each other even when it hurts.

———— ✦ ————

Prayer

God, thank You for pursuing my heart!
Thank You that even when I'm moving away, You're moving toward me.
I know that I can give this gift to others.
I choose to be someone who actively pursues connection with people today.
I give my life to pursue love and everything that comes with it.
That is what You do, Jesus; You go head over heels for love with each one of us.
Show me how I can make love my number one priority and pursuit.
Thank You, Jesus, for Your guidance and direction.

Reflection

1. How do you experience Jesus pursuing you in this season?

    _____
    _____
    _____
    _____

2. What does being pursued do for your heart? How has it changed you? If you have not been open to pursuit, what might your fears be about being pursued?

    _____
    _____
    _____
    _____

3. How does your pursuit of connection with God set you up to pursue connection in other relationships?

    _____
    _____
    _____
    _____

4. Are there friends or family members you might practice pursuing more this week?

    _____
    _____
    _____
    _____

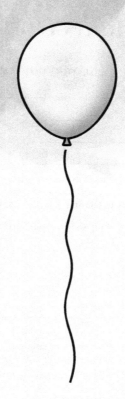

Day 49 – Ownership

OVERCOMING
THE FEAR OF LOSS

"Real security can only be found in that which can never be taken from you—your relationship with God."

Rick Warren

"Fear not, for I am with you; Be not dismayed, for I am your God. I will strengthen you, Yes, I will help you, I will uphold you with My righteous right hand."

Isaiah 41:10 NKJV

We all have different fears when it comes to our relationships, but they usually center around the fear that the more we love, the more we have to lose. There is no great love without great risk! We have a choice in how we respond to the fear of losing what we love most. One of the most powerful choices to gain tools is managing our own emotions and learning how to process loss and rejection so that it no longer has a foothold in our life. If this feels like a hard choice, God offers us help and comfort: "Fear not, for I am with you; be not dismayed, for I am your God. I will strengthen you. Yes, I will help you, I will uphold you with my righteous right hand" (Isaiah 41:10).

Fear is a destructive power in our relationship with ourselves, God, and others. Fear tries to get in the way of the intimacy we were designed for. Most of us are scared to death of being vulnerable in relationships, because we're afraid to lose the thing we love most. We are afraid of what will happen to us, instead of trusting ourselves to get us through and trusting we have all we need to bounce back. Deep down, we know that love is the only thing that will satisfy our hearts. Though we may fear losing it, it's far worse to never have it at all.

Imagine how hard it must have been for Mary to share with Joseph that she'd become pregnant by the Holy Spirit. Although she accepted the honor of her assignment wholeheartedly, I wonder if she worried what that assignment might cost her? Announcing to her fiancé that she was pregnant couldn't have been an easy conversation. She risked being rejected by Joseph, and once she had the baby, by her community as well.

She may have been facing that reality of spending her life in disgrace. By sharing her most vulnerable secret with Joseph, she risked everything. But the risk was worth it. God was with her and Joseph was afraid too. But God intervened, and Joseph didn't reject her. God can intervene for you as well!

***

Prayer

God, thank you that where I'm afraid of what I might lose,
You're excited about what I might gain.
When opening my heart feels scary,
I trust that You are the protector of my heart.
I choose to take a step toward connection today and allow my needs
to be met in my relationships.
You also bring redemption to each area of loss.
I know what is lost is not lost for good.
You are a redemptive Father and You have redemptive plans for everything.
Show me how to overcome the fear of any loss in my life.
Thank You, Jesus.

Reflection

1. Describe a situation in your life where vulnerability opened the door to deeper bonding and connection.

   _____

   _____

   _____

   _____

2. What made you feel safe or feel compelled to be vulnerable then?

   _____

   _____

   _____

   _____

3. What impact might it have on your relationships if you were more vulnerable with others?

   _____

   _____

   _____

   _____

4. What is an area you might need to grow in to establish a foundation in God's love where you feel safe and secure to be more vulnerable?

   _____

   _____

   _____

   _____

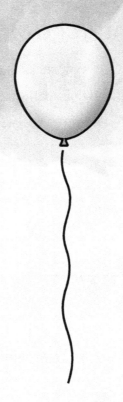

Day 50– Openness

VALIDATING
OTHERS

"Just like children, emotions heal when they are heard and validated."

Dr. Jill Bolte Taylor

"...the Lord does not see as man sees, for man looks at the outward appearance, but the Lord looks at the heart."

1 Samuel 16:7 NKJV

One of the keys to taking ownership for our lives and relationships is being okay with other people not being us. It might seem simple, but our fears are often triggered by what we don't know, or feel we cannot predict. So, when people start acting in ways we don't understand, or sharing opinions we do not agree with, we become fearful or frustrated. When we change our posture to be validating and curious about the differences, it helps us keep the respectful conversation going, and the relationship grows stronger. 1 Samuel 16:7 says, "...the Lord sees not as man sees: man looks on the outward appearance, but the Lord looks on the heart." We validate others when we value their heart even when their thoughts, feelings, or experiences are different from ours.

Any two people will always have experiences that have shaped them in ways that are different from each other. Respecting and valuing our differences protects our relationship. When we validate others, we communicate acceptance and trust even if we don't agree. Validation looks like being able to accurately reflect back to the person what they said, asking questions that seek to understand, practicing empathy, and taking the time to explore the thoughts, feelings, or experiences that led the person to think the way they do. When we communicate value for not just their opinion but the experiences that led them to their opinion, we set ourselves up for greater intimacy and a greater ability to meet each other's needs. If we ignore or invalidate each other, we immediately weaken the relationship.

We see this often play out harmfully in relationships where one person shares their feelings and the other says, "That is not logical; you shouldn't feel that way. Listen to all my reasons why you should feel differently..." Whether they meant to or not, the second person sent the message: "I am valuable and you are not. The way I process information is rational and the way you process information is not." The truth is that feelings tell the truth about someone's perception of a situation. They are not meant to tell us objective right or wrong. But if we do not take the time to understand feelings, we will have no power to solve or resolve them. If we do not take the time to value and understand someone's perception, we say they are not worthy of being understood and supported. Then neither person feels understood or has their needs met or resolved. If we can learn to value each other's differences by validating each other's thoughts, feelings, and experiences even when we don't understand them, we can protect and strengthen our relationship.

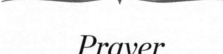

Prayer

Lord, thank You that You created my feelings and desire me to use them for good, to give me information and empower me. Thank You that in Your love, You validate my feelings, emotions and experiences. Allow my heart to rest knowing I do not need to defend my heart or my intentions to You. Create in me a heart to understand others, and be willing to sacrifice my desire to control or change their feelings and replace it with a desire to accept and love from them where they are at, even when they are having hard feelings. I want to be an agent of healing to demonstrate Your comfort to others. I choose to protect my relationships by deeply valuing the thoughts and experiences of others, even when I do not understand.

Reflection

1. Does validating someone else's feelings come easily to you?

   _____

   _____

   _____

   _____

2. Are there any fears you need to let go of to validate others better?

   _____

   _____

   _____

   _____

3. In what practical ways could you demonstrate value for others in conversations?

   _____

   _____

   _____

   _____

4. Think about the conversations in which you've felt most understood. What made them different?

   _____

   _____

   _____

   _____

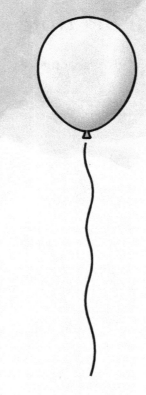

Day 51 – Ownership

OVERCOMING
THE FEAR OF PAIN

"Fear is the great enemy of intimacy. Fear makes us run away from each other or cling to each other but does not create true intimacy."

Henri Nouwen

If you've had a painful history with relationships, either in your family or other relationships, you're likely to have first-hand knowledge of how much it can hurt to be betrayed, disappointed, or abused by another person. It is natural to fear pain when we've experienced it in our past, but God always wants to write a different story about our future. He has a redemptive plan for us when it comes to relationships, and is committed to seeing it fulfilled! Psalm 56:3 says, "Whenever I am afraid, I will trust in you." We can trust Him in the midst of our fear!

The choice you make after you are hurt is the choice that is the hardest, but it shows where your love truly lies. Think of God. Adam and Eve hurt Him, but He put in place a plan for restoration. Peter betrayed Jesus, yet Jesus continued to make the choice to not fear the pain. What if Jesus had instead stayed stuck on the offense? What if He gave up on Peter and walked away? Peter would have never been the "rock" the entire church was built on. And what tremendous passion and fruit came from Peter's life and decision to serve God after he saw Jesus's commitment to him! Each of us has the same choice to make. Often, we are afraid we will be hurt again, but this cannot allow us to change our goal of connection to words and behaviors that demonstrate disconnection. Instead, with God's help, we can face our fears and continue to work toward fulfilling connections. We may need a healing journey, but if we keep choosing love, God is faithful to deliver us from our fears.

Fear of pain will often impact how vulnerable we're willing to be in relationships. We will also be more likely to try to avoid pain in the way we communicate. This can look like being passive (pretending your feelings don't matter so the other person doesn't get upset), becoming overly emotional (trying to control the other person by manipulating them into a kind response) or becoming aggressive (hurting them before they hurt you). None of these, or any other pain-avoidance strategies, will actually help you avoid pain long term. Instead, we must take responsibility and ownership of our past, and do the best we can to move in awareness and compassion toward our fear, instead of reacting out of fear in ways that only continue to damage our lives. If we can do this, we can take the steps to get our greatest need for love met in relationships.

———— ✦ ————

Prayer

God, thank You for understanding the pain.
Thank You for being with me in the midst of pain,
and with me as I overcome my fear of experiencing it again.
Thank You that You're faithful to lead me into a place of victory
where my heart is free to experience the love available to me.
You overcame so much in life and are perfectly positioned to help me overcome it.
When I am experiencing pain or the fear of pain,
teach me to look into Your wonderful eyes and get what I need.
I want to overcome with You, Jesus.

Reflection

1. Assess your usual reactions to hard conversations. What pain-
    avoidance strategies do you use?

    _____

    _____

    _____

    _____

2. What is one positive action you can start to develop as a habit that
    would serve you better than pain-avoidance strategies?

    _____

    _____

    _____

    _____

3. Where in the Bible does God demonstrate restoration or
    breakthrough after pain?

    _____

    _____

    _____

    _____

4. How would your relationships change if you overcame the fear of
    pain and were connected to what God has for you in relationships?

    _____

    _____

    _____

    _____

Day 52– Openness

COMMUNICATING YOUR DESIRES

"A desire to be observed, considered, esteemed, praised, beloved, and admired by his fellows is one of the earliest as well as the keenest dispositions discovered in the heart of man."

John Adams

"Hope deferred makes the heart sick,
But when the desire comes, it is a tree of life."

Proverbs 13:12 NKJV

esires are the hopes and dreams that God has placed in our heart for ourselves and our relationships. It can be the desire to get married, have children, have a shared mission, do a round-the-world trip together, or a hundred other things. Proverbs 13:12 says, "Hope deferred makes the heart sick, But when the desire comes, it is a tree of life." When we recognize that our desires are from our Father God, and value and communicate the desires of our heart to others, we plant seeds that become trees of life in our relationships.

Communicating our desires requires as much, if not more, vulnerability than communicating our needs. Just like with our needs, we first have to value ourselves and our dreams and desires in order to communicate them to somebody else. If we're used to rejecting ownership of our dreams, we treat them like they don't matter, and do not give them space to grow and develop in our lives. If people do not own their dreams, they tend to hide their desires for fear of having them ridiculed, or they try to manipulate and control others into fulfilling them. Owners know what they desire and how to communicate it. If we refuse to own and value our own dreams, we cannot expect anyone else to value them. Communicating our desires is so important because they're a window to be known on an even deeper level than when we share our needs. Similarly, when someone shares a desire with us, they are not sharing random information; they are trusting us with a sacred piece of their heart. Sharing a need builds trust, but sharing a dream and desire builds intimacy.

In Psalm 21, we see David express his joy at the desire of his heart being fulfilled. "The king shall have joy in your strength, O Lord, and in your salvation how greatly shall he rejoice! You have given him his heart's desire, and have not withheld the request of his lips." Jesus tells us in John 15 that if we abide in Him, we can ask what we desire and it will be done for us. When we recognize that it is God's desire that we not only have what we need, but that our desires are fulfilled, we can learn to communicate these desires to Him freely, and to others as well.

Prayer

*God, I praise You that You have placed desires in my heart
and want to give them to me! I know that these are not meant to remain hidden,
but to be communicated to people who care about me.
Thank You that as I communicate my desires,
I create the opportunity for them to be met, supported, and nourished.
I choose to believe that all the dreams You have given to me
were given to me for a reason, and I can partner with You
and others to see them fulfilled. Allow me to be an agent of change
to help other's dreams and desires come true as well.*

Reflection

1. How easy do you find it to dream? Is this always how it has been or has something changed that?

   _____

   _____

   _____

   _____

2. How do you feel when you see one of your desires has been fulfilled?

   _____

   _____

   _____

   _____

3. What could be getting in the way of communicating your desires or hearing and fulfilling the desires of others?

   _____

   _____

   _____

   _____

4. What is a low-stakes desire that you can communicate to God or someone else today?

   _____

   _____

   _____

   _____

Day 53– Ownership

THE ROOT OF UNHEALTHY COMMUNICATION IS LACK OF OWNERSHIP

"To be passive is to let others decide for you. To be aggressive is to decide for others. To be assertive is to decide for yourself. And to trust that there is enough, that you are enough."

Dr. Edith Eva Eger

"...Speaking the truth in love, may (we) grow up in all things into Him who is the head—Christ."

Ephesians 4:15 NKJV

*L*earning new skills for communication can feel like a long journey at times. Sometimes, people want to control the journey, but when they do, they shift the focus away from taking ownership of themselves. People often ask us, "What if the person I'm talking to doesn't follow the rules?" They're wondering how they apply the communication skills they've learned when they're in a conversation with a powerless person. My encouragement is this: if you are doing the same math problem and do not like the result, you only need to change one number to get a better result! That number is you! Ephesians 4:15 encourages us to "speak the truth in love," so that all may grow in maturity. This doesn't mean we should try to control others, but it does mean we get to control ourselves and set standards in our relationships.

When we're struggling to face the truth inside us, and can't articulate our feelings, needs, and desires, we end up communicating confusing and inaccurate information to each other. This is what's happening when we're communicating with a person who can't take ownership. If they're aggressive, their core belief is: "I matter and you don't." They get what they want by being the scariest person in the room. If they're passive-aggressive, their core belief is: "You matter...but you should think I matter and feel bad you didn't do what I wanted!" They control through manipulation and subtle forms of punishment. If they're passive, their core belief is: "You matter and I don't," and they will avoid sharing their own thoughts and feelings. As we learn to take ownership for ourselves, we start to become better, assertive communicators. Our core belief is:

226

"You matter and so do I." We can refuse to have conversations in which both people don't have high, equal value.

The quickest way to encourage someone to take ownership when they are upset is to ask them what they need. Most often, they will not know right away, but the fact that they do not know challenges them to get in touch with their feelings, desires, and needs and learn to communicate with them. This is a great place to start in setting new standards in your relationships, and a great question to ask ourselves, too.

Prayer

God, thank You for designing each of us free and powerful
to make decisions as owners of our own lives. When I come across people who
do not take ownership of their lives and emotions, I choose to retain ownership of mine.
I choose to love and to invite others to do the same. You have shown me
time and time again how to remain empowered through your word.
I look to You for the same approach in each area of my life.
I am able to make decisions with Your help and I can lead healthy relationships
with You. Thank You, God, for all of Your care and support.

Reflection

1. In hard conversations, do you tend to react more in passive, passive-aggressive, or aggressive ways?

   _____

   _____

   _____

   _____

2. What is the fear that drives you to react that way?

   _____

   _____

   _____

   _____

3. What is a truth God has for you in His word that can replace that fear?

   _____

   _____

   _____

   _____

4. What is a phrase and an action you might use in an upcoming conversation that would demonstrate that you have a high and equal value for yourself and others?

   _____

   _____

   _____

   _____

Day 54— Openness

MAKING YOUR VISION PLAIN

"A common vision can unite people of very different temperaments."

Timothy Keller

"Where there is no vision, the people perish: but he that keepeth the law, happy is he."

Proverbs 29:18 KJV

reat relationships have great vision that is communicated, understood, and provides direction for those involved. You can have a vision for your marriage, your family, your friendships, and even your work relationships. Vision sets the course for your relationship, defines your priorities, and points you toward shared goals. It also helps you know when you can celebrate the hard work you put in to achieve those goals together! If we want to preserve unity in our relationships, a shared vision is important. Proverbs 29:18 says, "Where there is no vision, the people perish." This tells us that in order to keep persevering toward a goal, we must know where we're going. Otherwise, we're too easily knocked off course. Defining vision personally and with others is a great way to be intentional with our lives and relationships.

It is important to take ownership to create and refine your vision. No one else can do this for you. We also have to do this in our key relationships. When we do, it keeps us connected and aware of where we are at, as well as where we are heading together. If you have ever heard of people saying they "grew apart," what they mean is that they chose little by little, day by day, not to take ownership to check in and assess where the relationship was at, and where it was heading.

This means we should actively pursue each other's personal vision, dreams, identity, and calling. Remembering that our highest calling is love, we can then adapt, shift, and reassess our personal vision, dreams, identity, and calling to see how we might collaborate and encourage each other. Ally drastically shifted how her "calling" looked when she met

230

Jeremy. Part of this was out of necessity. She was working one hundred hours a week at the time, and it was hard to build a relationship if she was not willing to adapt and shift toward a new definition of her calling. She felt empowering Jeremy became a big part of her calling and feels that calling has allowed her to know God in deeper, more profound ways than ever before. Sometimes, having shared vision just means setting goals for your relationship. Your vision might be to help each other become the best you can be by offering encouragement or reminding each other of who you are when things are hard. People are a blessing on this journey of life, and making sure we're communicating about shared vision helps us move toward both personal and shared goals.

Prayer

God, thank You for Your vision for my life and for each of my relationships.
I choose to connect with vision and actively move toward it.
I live in great expectation as I partner with You to create practices and habits
that are in alignment with everything You dream for me in this area.
Your wisdom and perspective are available to me through the Holy Spirit.
Thank You, Jesus, for showing the world the vision that You carry in your heart.
I desire to sit close to You and pull from Your vision for my life and in turn
create a vision that is clear and plain for everyone to walk on.

Reflection

1. Are there elements of yourself and God's vision for your life
    that you feel you have lost?

    _____

    _____

    _____

    _____

2. What would it take to move one step closer to God's vision for
    your life today?

    _____

    _____

    _____

    _____

3. Consider writing a vision statement for your contribution to your
    closest relationships. What would it include?

    _____

    _____

    _____

    _____

4. Do you know of someone else who seems to have lost their vision?
    What can you do to encourage them today?

    _____

    _____

    _____

    _____

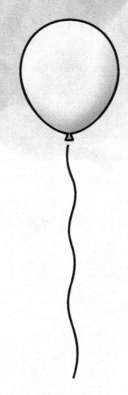

Day 55 – Ownership

CLEARLY
COMMUNICATING
NEEDS

*"Until we can receive with an open heart, we're never really giving
with an open heart. When we attach judgment to receiving help,
we knowingly or unknowingly attach judgment to giving help."*

Dr. Brene

> *"Let nothing be done through selfish ambition or conceit, but in lowliness of mind let each esteem others better than himself."*
>
> Philippians 2:3 NKVJ

*I*magine a newlywed couple moving into their new home. She is used to living by herself and values tidiness because she loves to entertain visitors. He was in a flatshare with four other guys, and considers tidiness a low priority compared to having fun. After a couple of months of mutual irritation, they sit down and talk about their needs. Instead of name-calling ("you slob," "you neat freak"), or blaming the other for their frustration, she is able to say, "I don't know why I need this, but I need the living room tidy." He then has a choice to meet that need, even though it's not his "normal." As they continue the conversation, they realize they have a shared desire to entertain and have fun in their home. His need is met, and so is hers, but they could only get there by giving each other the space to express their need without judgment.

The faster we can get to "what do you need?" in a conversation, the faster we can start doing something about it! Unfortunately, most people aren't used to being listened to, and many aren't used to listening! To build trust in relationships, we must learn to articulate our own needs clearly, and also to listen well to others in order to understand what they need. Philippians 2:3 encourages us to "let nothing be done through selfish ambition or conceit, but in lowliness of mind let each esteem others better than himself." We fulfill this scripture when we value the needs of others enough to prioritize taking the time to understand them.

One of the things that trips a lot of us up is we're not used to knowing what we need or how to communicate it. Also, we have trouble recognizing that our needs are important just because they exist. We think we have to present a solid case for someone to help us, agree with us, or change for us. If we think all of our needs have to be perfectly rational according to some logic, we will always find a way to invalidate our own needs. If we recognize that our needs exist regardless of whether we can justify them, we learn to understand them, value them, communicate them, and give others the opportunity to meet them. In the same way, when we value the needs of others even when we don't understand them, we're telling someone else, "I don't need this to have a solid case or a perfect rationale. I value your needs and want to try to meet them."

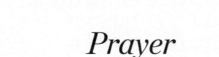

Prayer

God, thank You that You designed me for love,
and for my needs to be met in healthy relationships.
I know that if I want my needs to be met, I need to communicate them.
I commit to being quick to communicate my needs in my closest relationships.
Jesus even communicated Your needs to maintain and grow connection.
I love that You were vulnerable enough to communicate Your needs.
Thank You for showing me what is right and what I should do.
Thank You for modeling this. I will follow You and communicate my needs
to build and grow in connection.

Reflection

1. Describe a recent hard conversation. Were you asking yourself
    what you needed?

    _____

    _____

    _____

    _____

2. Consider reaching out to the other person and asking them
    what their needs are.

    _____

    _____

    _____

    _____

3. Consider words or phrases you could use to validate both your
    needs and theirs.

    _____

    _____

    _____

    _____

4. Are there people who come to you often complaining or upset that
    you might try asking, "What do you need?" instead of trying to
    calm them or give them advice?

    _____

    _____

    _____

    _____

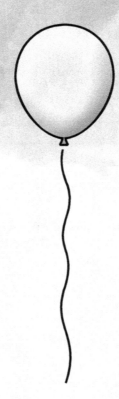

Day 56— Openness

RECIPROCAL
RELATIONSHIPS

*"There is one word which may serve as a rule of practice
for all one's life—reciprocity."*

Confucius

"Jesus said to him, 'You shall love the Lord your God with all your heart, with all your soul, and with all your mind.' This is the first and great commandment. And the second is like it: 'You shall love your neighbor as yourself.'"

Matthew 22:37-39 NKJV

The healthiest relationships are built on the principle of reciprocity. This means that I take ownership of my own life, including my happiness, my pain, my healing, and my gifts, and so do you. Then, as we share our lives with each other, we're both able to meet each other's needs, support each other through pain, and share joy together. We both have resources to give because we've been faithful to cultivate them in our own lives. Matthew 22:39 says, "You shall love your neighbor as yourself." This means that when we take responsibility for our own needs, and learn to love ourselves, we have what we need to love others. When two people do this, we have a reciprocal relationship.

Imagine you have a neighbor who takes no ownership for their yard. It's full of garbage, the lawn has never been mowed, and the vegetable beds have never been given fresh compost. Your neighbor looks over at your neat row of vegetables and asks for a few carrots. You give them to him. The next day he asks for more. You suggest he plant his own carrots, but he says nothing grows in his garden. The next day he asks for more, and you tell him if you keep giving him your vegetables, there will not be enough for you. He becomes angry, thinking it is unfair you have so much and are withholding it from him. The whole relationship blows up because he started to think you were the owner of the food that would sustain him, instead of you encouraging him and teaching him to learn to cultivate a garden to meet his own needs. But what if your neighbor also had a beautiful, well-tended garden? What if you could share your harvest, giving each of you a wider variety? What if you could talk about your passion for gardening, share stories and secrets? Relationships work best when both people know they're responsible for their own garden, and choose to share their lives with each other from this place.

Each of our lives is a garden given to us by God. It's full of natural resources and potential, but only when we tend it do we see it flourish. In an unhealthy situation, we look over the fence and expect someone else to tend our garden, or over-share what is in our garden, instead of helping someone learn to tend to their garden. When we're healthy, we realize that only we are responsible to care for our garden and eat from its fruit. Nobody else has that responsibility. When we diligently manage what is ours, we reap a harvest in our own lives that will nourish us. Once we've done this, we have something good to offer others. Yes, you will still come to the relationship with needs and participate in meeting each other's needs, but each will come from a fruitful place of having something to give.

Prayer

*I enter into peace and joy when I recognize relationships thrive
when two people embrace their individual responsibility.
Thank You that my part is to cultivate the resources of my life,
manage my boundaries, and keep loving.
I want to allow others to cultivate their resources well by upholding boundaries
and pointing them to You and Your unlimited resources!
Open my eyes to see the resources I have available to me,
and to look to You as the fulfiller of my needs first.
Let me share with others out of abundance, not pressure or unhealthy guilt.
I trust that as I take the steps You put before me,
I will build strong and healthy connections.*

Reflection

1. In which relationships in your life do you feel both people are prioritizing the relationship?

    _____
    _____
    _____
    _____

2. Do you have any relationships in which you feel people are relating to you as a consumer?

    _____
    _____
    _____
    _____

3. What might be a first step to start to draw some boundaries with them?

    _____
    _____
    _____
    _____

4. Does your allocation of time to different relationships reflect your true priorities?

    _____
    _____
    _____
    _____

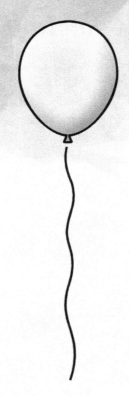

Day 57 – Ownership

COMMUNICATING
THE GIFT OF LOVE

*"God bestows His blessings without discrimination.
The followers of Jesus are children of God, and they should manifest
the family likeness by doing good to all, even to those
who deserve the opposite."*

F.F. Bruce

"But I say to you, love your enemies, bless those who curse you, do good to those who hate you, and pray for those who spitefully use you and persecute you, that you may be sons of your Father in heaven; for He makes His sun rise on the evil and on the good, and sends rain on the just and on the unjust."

Matthew 22:37-39 NKJV

Your affection is a precious gift that you choose to give others. Choosing to share this gift is about you recognizing that you are the owner of you, and nobody else. That includes how you maintain your love toward others. You can give your gifts of affection based on your priorities and nobody else's actions. 2 Corinthians 9:7-8 reminds us that God loves a cheerful giver who gives freely knowing God sufficiently and abundantly provides to us. We are free to give gifts of affection when we embrace healthy communication.

We both have found that giving a free gift of love resolves many relational conflicts and issues before they even start. Let's say one person is upset and voices that frustration. They may even use manipulation or blame, but instead of reacting, the second person takes ownership of their response, stays calm, and simply asks what the upset person needs. An argument requires two people to participate, and if one does not engage in the argument and instead focuses on responding as a teammate, giving love, compassion, and listening, things tend to resolve very quickly. In healthy relationships, people take turns offering this when the other is hurt, has an unmet need, or is tired and cranky.

It never ceases to amaze us that Jesus never lost His temper and blamed mankind for "making Him" have to come and die to save them. He never said, "This is all your fault," or, "I have every right to be upset with you all. I am getting tortured because of your sin and bad choices." He never said, "Do you know how terrible earth is? I wish I never met you and I wish I never came here." Jesus shows us that offering free gifts of undeserved love is one of the biggest keys to restore, heal, and nurture any relationship. Offering anger and retaliation was not something he demonstrated. A free gift of affection is based on our choice to nurture a healthy relationship, not based on what someone else has done or will do. Let's demonstrate that we have full ownership of our love and our actions, like Jesus. By taking ownership of our choices and making choices to love, we get to be a demonstration of a higher standard of love to those around us.

Prayer

God, thank You for creating us to give and receive affection.
I choose to love well by offering my affection as a free gift to my friends and family.
I choose to be generous with my affection,
knowing that I'm representing Your heart as I do.
I thank You that as I freely receive love, I have the privilege to give it away.
I will communicate the gift of love that You have given me.
Your love is the greatest gift that you gave the earth.
I want to know about Your love fully so I can become the person of love
that You desire me to be. Thank You, God,
for being so loving.

Reflection

1. Is it easy or difficult to freely express affection in your family and community?

   _____

   _____

   _____

   _____

2. Who might you look to as a model for how to improve your ability to give and receive gifts of affection?

   _____

   _____

   _____

   _____

3. What do they do differently and how might you start to emulate their approach?

   _____

   _____

   _____

   _____

4. Where could you choose to give the gift of affection freely today? It could be a text message, an encouraging call, a small gift, or inviting someone to spend time with you.

   _____

   _____

   _____

   _____

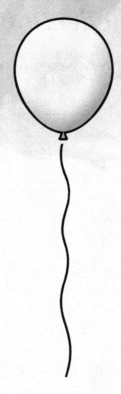

AGREEING TO DISAGREE

"The difference between successful people and really successful people is that really successful people say no to almost everything."

Warren Buffett

"So I sent messengers to them, saying,
'I am doing a great work, so that I cannot come down.
Why should the work cease while I leave it
and go down to you?'

Nehemiah 6:3 NKJV

Setting boundaries requires us to make choices, regardless of whether or not somebody agrees with them. When Nehemiah was building the walls of Jerusalem, his enemies sent a message asking him to come and speak to him at least four times, but Nehemiah kept agreeing to disagree by setting boundaries according to his priorities. He said, "I am doing a great work, so that I cannot come down" (Nehemiah 6:3). If we don't learn to take ownership of our time and how we spend it, we'll find ourselves reacting to others instead of taking ownership of our choices. When we set boundaries, we make choices based on our priorities, not on the needs of others. This means we'll come up against a disagreement from time to time.

When you're faithful to cultivate your own garden, and have produced attractive and nourishing fruit, you'll find that people will start to notice. If you don't set boundaries around what people can and cannot take from you, it's like leaving the yard gate open and letting the whole neighborhood take what they want. Sooner or later, your trees will be bare and when you want to offer the people closest to you some of your fruit, you will have nothing left to give. Instead, decide in advance what you are willing to give and who you are willing to give it to. Your priorities should be your family, friends, and people closest to you. You may then want to give to others in a different way. For example, we share the fruit of our life with strangers through books and podcasts, but our family gets most of our face-to-face time.

246

One of our friends had a very difficult relationship with a family member. They found themselves always neglecting their wants and needs, while bending over backwards to meet the desires and needs of one member. Finally, they realized they were tending someone else's garden full time, but reaping none of the harvest, which left them with a lot of resentment and bitterness. We encouraged this person to set boundaries and start by tending their garden, and then see if they had extra to share. The family member did not like this, and became very angry that they stopped getting free labor in their own garden. But what happened next was amazing! Seeing our friend's example, the family member then realized that she was not tending to her garden, and that is why she felt others should tend to it, because she had no time left for it. This revelation broke a generational pattern in the family and brought healthy alignment to everyone. The family could now focus on what they did best, and give to each other from abundance and not lack or compulsion.

Prayer

How amazing that You, God, created each of us uniquely, with different passions and points of view. It is a mystery at times how You have made us all in your image, yet with such diversity as well. Help me ponder and understand where I might see glimpses of You in others who are not like me. Where I've found disagreements difficult in the past, I now embrace them as an opportunity to demonstrate love. I choose to set a new standard in my relationships that allows both parties to be responsible to protect connection, even when we disagree.

Reflection

1. Who are the most important people you want to give your time, energy, love, and life to?

    _____

    _____

    _____

    _____

2. Do any relationships come to mind that are taking more from you than you'd like to give?

    _____

    _____

    _____

    _____

3. Are you comfortable saying "no" when something or someone is not a priority to you?

    _____

    _____

    _____

    _____

4. If not, what are your fears about saying no?

    _____

    _____

    _____

    _____

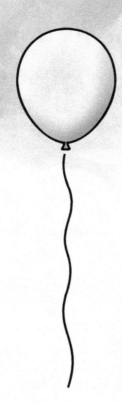

Day 59 – Ownership

YOU CANNOT OWN
WHAT BELONGS
TO SOMEONE ELSE

"You are not a victim. You can control your reactions.
You do have a choice."

Dr. Caroline Leaf

*"And do not be conformed to this world,
but be transformed by the renewing of your mind,
that you may prove what is that good and acceptable
and perfect will of God."*

Romans 12:2 NKJV

Each of us is responsible for creating the world we live in, and for our own happiness. We have heard it said that "every problem has an owner." People who have a victim mentality are constantly looking for other people to be their emotional owner. Caring people often jump in to try to rescue them, only to find weeks, months, or years later that their help has not created any change. Meanwhile, people with a victim mentality feel victimized again when people they want to take ownership of can't or don't do exactly what they want. Often, then they will blame and try to shame the "rescuer" into redoubling their effort to help. This will never help them, as no one can say they own something that is simply not theirs.

Sometimes, caring people get stuck in this dynamic. Ally worked with many people who had a victim mentality, and she herself did as a teen, so it was easy for her to recognize. There is a big difference between people who are victims of bad situations and need support to get through that hard time, and people who live from a victim mentality. This difference comes back to ownership. As a therapist, Ally met many people who thought the role of a therapist was to "fix" them, their child, or their relationship. As if the therapist in one hour could fully take ownership for a problem they do not participate in for the other 167 hours of the week. In truth, no therapist can magically take ownership for and then fix your problem. But a good therapist will share general wisdom and solutions, and then facilitate and unlock your ability to take ownership and find the solutions that work for you and your relationship.

Instead of jumping into "rescue" mode when we hear a sad story, it is much better to offer both compassion and support a person to be their own owner. We do this by asking good questions instead of offering solutions that may make us feel good and helpful, but rarely help others take ownership. For example, a great response is, "Wow, that sounds so tough. What are you going to do about that? What have you tried already? What else could you try?" These questions demonstrate you know you are not responsible for the other person, and help them take responsibility. Sometimes, this dynamic is flipped and we encounter a "rescuer" who thinks they can take ownership of our bad situation. It is important to also reassure them we do not need rescuing. A true owner is not tempted to label people as "victim," "bad guy," or "rescuer" and they are unwilling to play these roles themselves.

Prayer

God, thank You for loving relationships that cultivate safety,
mutual respect, and trust. I choose to be an owner today,
and let go of trying to own problems and people You didn't call me to own.
I release these to You and back to their owner. I embrace the emotional freedom
of not trying to solve problems I am not the owner of.
Holy Spirit, search to the ends of the earth to bring me the best solutions
to glorify Jesus and bring His will to the earth and in my relationships.
I want to establish all of these healthy patterns of connection that You give.
Thank You, God, for proving such a wonderful roadmap
for me to thrive in life.

Reflection

1. When you consider the roles of victim, bad guy, and rescuer, where do you see yourself?

    _____

    _____

    _____

    _____

2. How does your understanding of being an owner challenge your current role?

    _____

    _____

    _____

    _____

3. Are there any other relationships where you take responsibility for someone else's happiness?

    _____

    _____

    _____

    _____

4. How could you start to ask responsibility questions that encourage long-term growth?

    _____

    _____

    _____

    _____

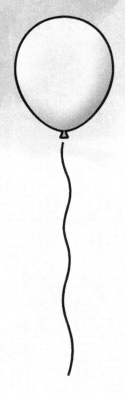

Day 60~ Openness

AGREEMENT
ISN'T THE GOAL

*"Families who have strong and healthy communication skills
can weather significant challenges and remain intact.
Those with limited effective communication skills
are vulnerable to the challenges of life pulling them apart."*

Ellen Miley Perry

253

When we communicate, it may feel like agreement is the goal, but making agreement the goal of communication actually puts impossible pressure on it. We're all different, with different personalities, thoughts, feelings, and viewpoints. We can't guarantee that we'll always reach an agreement when we communicate, but if we commit to staying connected, we can work toward the more realistic goal of understanding and fully accepting each other instead. 1 Corinthians 13:7 tells us that "love always protects, always trusts, always hopes, always perseveres." Our goal in communication is to protect the other person's right to be themselves, to trust their heart, and to persevere in hope toward a place of understanding each other.

We all have disagreements from time to time! If two people never disagree, then one or both of them are hiding their true opinions or feelings. If the goal is always agreement, it follows that one person will always have to disappear in order to reach that goal. Disagreements do not need to lead to conflict; however, they can lead to conflict, and conflict is never fun. When we prioritize our connection over being right or winning arguments, and keep pursuing the goal of understanding, most conflicts are worked out in the momentum of staying connected. But, even if the conflict isn't resolved, at least the relationship will be protected. Believe it or not, it is possible to stay connected to someone with whom you profoundly disagree!

This all comes down to creating a hierarchy of priorities. The question to ask is this: is getting what you want more important than maintaining a healthy relationship? Ally has incredibly strong convictions about not eating animal meat. She has very strong feelings about not killing animals. Jeremy has no such conviction. Meat is a big part of his culture and valued highly in the community where he grew up. This could easily escalate to one of them trying to control the other in their ideals. But this disagreement has never caused a single relational problem. Both of us respect that the other can take ownership for their diet, and is allowed to make their own choices. We do not get to choose what the other eats, but we do get to own how this difference impacts how we show up in our relationship. Because of this, no conflict ever develops. As we express this to each other, we strengthen our relationships into a more powerful connection because we can disagree and still allow each other to be ourselves.

Prayer

God, thank You for the power of agreement and even when it is not there,
I have full ownership of how I choose to love.
Thank You that you modeled this for me by allowing me to have free will
instead of controlling me into salvation. In my closest relationships,
I choose to intentionally set goals for communication.
I commit to working with others to establish agreement on these goals
and move toward creating a healthy environment of mutual respect.
When I enter into a disagreement, help me to hold fast to the most important things:
relationships, connection, and love.

Reflection

1. Are there things you think God values more than agreement in conversations?

   _____

   _____

   _____

   _____

2. Are there things you value more than agreement in difficult conversations?

   _____

   _____

   _____

   _____

3. Create a list of helpful goals you can set when trying to reach an agreement in communication?

   _____

   _____

   _____

   _____

4. What might healthy communication during disagreements look like for you?

   _____

   _____

   _____

   _____

Day 61 – Ownership

CREATING SAFETY IN HARD CONVERSATIONS

"Constant kindness can accomplish much.
As the sun makes ice melt, kindness causes misunderstanding,
mistrust, and hostility to evaporate."

Dr. Albert Schweitzer

"The Lord will rescue me from every evil attack and will bring me safely to His heavenly kingdom. To Him be the glory forever and ever. Amen."

2 Timothy 4:17 NIV

Jesus always created a space of safety around Him by the kinds of conversations He had with people. His disciples show us that they felt free to be themselves around Jesus by the way they asked questions, how John leaned against his chest, and how Peter was free to speak his mind and make mistakes. In fact, Jesus felt so safe to Peter that when he saw Him walking on water, he said, "Lord, if it's you...tell me to come to you on the water" (Matthew 14:28) Peter knew that if Jesus was there, he was perfectly safe even in the most unlikely of situations. The circumstance didn't matter; the other people didn't matter—t he knew that within that relationship, he was safe.

The best conversations happen when both people feel safe. Creating a sense of safety in our relationships is a great way to ensure both people feel free to express their hearts in vulnerability and honesty. When love is strong in a relationship, you will see fear leaving and being replaced with courage, freedom, and safety. 2 Timothy 4:17 says, "The Lord will rescue me from every evil attack and will bring me safely to His heavenly kingdom." Our hearts are perfectly safe in the love of God, and as a result we get to create safe places for the hearts of others, too.

If we can successfully send the message that we love someone, we immediately increase their sense of safety. The more we're assured of unconditional love, and can assure others, the safer we will feel. Conditional love and acceptance say that we are willing to de-value the relationship and pull away from our connection under certain circumstances. In this case, when somebody scares us, we retreat or withdraw from them. This produces more fear and we increase the distance between us. However, when we commit to love and connection, we protect each other's freedom and create a safe place to be ourselves. Only people who can own their choices can create a safe space to know and be known intimately. They say, "I can be me around you and you can be you around me. We don't need to control each other, and we don't want to control each other. We have a mutual agreement of respect and honor in which we both work to protect our relationship." We can build relationships of safety by letting people be fully themselves around us, with no judgment and no expectation.

Prayer

God, thank You for providing a safe place for my heart.
Thank You for giving me the power to create safe spaces for others
to feel free to be fully themselves. As I am known and loved by You,
I choose to create opportunities for people to be known and loved by me.
Show me how to defuse any attack in conversation and create a home of peace and safely.
I look to You as I enter into each house and let my peace go out from me.
I want to establish a home of peace and safety.
You are a wonderful teacher.

Reflection

1. Describe a conversation you have had where you felt safe and able
    to be your true self. What was said and done by the other person
    that contributed to you feeling safe?

    _____

    _____

    _____

    _____

2. What are your "non-negotiables" in your relationships concerning
    how you're treated?

    _____

    _____

    _____

    _____

3. Do you communicate these freely and openly to others?

    _____

    _____

    _____

    _____

4. How do you intentionally create places of safety for others?

    _____

    _____

    _____

    _____

Day 62~ Openness

BUILDING
TRUST

"Trust is the fruit of a relationship in which you know you are loved."

William P. Young

"May the God of hope fill you with all joy and peace as you trust in Him, so that you may overflow with hope by the power of the Holy Spirit."

Romans 15:13 NIV

As we grow up in an imperfect world with imperfect people, our trust invariably gets broken or damaged along the way. If you're looking to break a pattern of mistrust and powerlessness, the first steps are learning to own your lack of trust and communicate your needs. Romans 15:13 says, "May the God of hope fill you with all joy and peace as you trust in Him, so that you may overflow with hope by the power of the Holy Spirit." The best place to build trust is with Father God, who is faithful to fill you with hope and transformative power to rebuild trust in your relationships with people. As we get good at recognizing what's going on inside us and taking ownership, we can then share that information with others. As they get good at listening to us and meeting our needs (and we do the same for them), trust is built in our relationships.

At the very beginning of our relationship, Ally had some trust issues. She would misinterpret things and react by withdrawing, instead of caring and connecting. She knew this was hurtful to Jeremy, as he had done nothing wrong. She very quickly realized she had to take ownership, or else she was constantly going to be sowing bad fruit from the past into a relationship she really valued. Instead of expecting Jeremy to know how to stop her from being triggered, she worked diligently to share what was going on in her mind and heart. This helped both parties know which step of ownership they could take to help the situation.

Ally took ownership to reduce the length and intensity of her reactions, and apologize when it impacted the relationship or day. Her goal was to make herself "trigger-proof" by turning on the "safety lock" in her heart through her relationship with God, whom she trusted fully. Jeremy took ownership for demonstrating care, grace, and trustworthiness, regardless of what Ally did. He did not take ownership for her fear or lack of trust, which kept him from falling into defensive, blaming, or angry reactions. With each owning what they could, the trust issue quickly disappeared and has not come up since. Now, we know this is not the normal timeline for most people starting their journey of trust and ownership, so be patient with yourself! This is, however, the fruit of a decade of work both of us put in before we met each other. Had we met a decade ago, it would have possibly taken years of practice and regrouping to overcome this problem. Still, no matter where we are in our journey, we can all make the choice to say, "I will trust you. You don't control my trust; I do." This frees us to be fully ourselves, and take responsibility for our part of the trust cycle.

Prayer

God, thank You that trust is built on the exchange of truth.
Thank You that I can develop trust by speaking the truth,
being a person of my words and being consistent in my actions.
I am empowered by Jesus's example to not allow fear of betrayal or punishment
to hinder my decision to love. You are the source of love that never runs dry
and You can always be trusted. You empower me to have and give more
than enough love and trust. Today, I choose to prioritize
developing trust in my relationships.

Reflection

1. Consider Jesus knowing He would be betrayed. What do you think empowered Him to be able to value trust more than shame, condemnation, or fear?

    _____

    _____

    _____

    _____

2. What do you think is the most powerful thing you can do to build trust in a relationship?

    _____

    _____

    _____

    _____

3. Is there a relationship in your life that you could apply this lens of trust to?

    _____

    _____

    _____

    _____

4. How could trusting someone regardless of what they may or may not do allow you to access increased freedom in your thoughts, spiritual walk, and relationships?

    _____

    _____

    _____

    _____

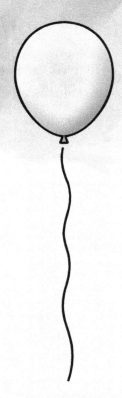

Day 63— Ownership

COMMUNICATING
RESPECTFULLY

*"If you have some respect for people as they are, you can be more
effective in helping them to become better than they are."*

Dr. John W. Gardner

*"For you, brethren, have been called to liberty;
only do not use liberty as an opportunity for the flesh,
but through love serve one another."*

Galatians 5:13 NKJV

ave you ever wondered what separates great communication from bad communication in relationships? It's not about the words you use, the eloquence of your delivery, or whether or not your message was understood. This should take some pressure off! Great communication in relationships rests on one thing: mutual respect. Respectful communication means that both people in the conversation were treated in line with the belief that they have high and equal value. Galatians 5:13 reminds us to use our freedom to serve each other, not ourselves. We do this when we choose to show respect.

Assertive communicators take responsibility for their part in creating respectful conversations. The goal of the conversation is that each person shares honestly about what's going on for them. So, if respect isn't happening, we can steer the conversation by saying, "Hey, this conversation doesn't feel respectful. I'm happy to continue when you're ready to show me your heart instead of telling me about me." Conversations aren't respectful when either person's thoughts, feelings, and needs are being devalued. If this is happening, we have to take the ownership to stop the conversation and communicate to the other person that until respect is restored, we won't continue participating in the conversation. This may be difficult if we're stuck in a cycle of doing things a certain way, but when we choose to fight for change, we take control of what we are and aren't willing to do, and invite others to take ownership of the relationship too.

Jesus demonstrated respect in conversations, even when dealing with people society did not respect. Tax collectors, thieves, the woman at the well, and the woman who was about to be stoned for adultery were some of them. He pulled them up into his level of respect, instead of degrading himself by choosing to disrespect them. This created an opportunity for those he encountered to step into greater self-respect and change. The best place to start the process of respecting others is respecting ourselves. If we allow anger, criticism, and lack of respect from ourselves in our mind and heart, this will inevitably spill out toward others. We can all take ownership for the level of respect we have toward ourselves and in our relationships. As we do, we provide opportunities for the relationship to grow.

Prayer

God, thank You that each person is created in Your image and worthy of respect.
Thank You that You are a model of respectful communication and You choose
to communicate respectfully with me when I sin or make mistakes,
even though You do not have to.
I choose to be someone who shines Your light and demonstrates Your character
by being respectful in how I talk to people and how I talk about them.
When I am not respected in this way, I choose to remember
that Jesus was not always respected either.
I choose to see how You can lead me through a response
while creating healthy boundaries around my conversations.

Reflection

1. Do you tend to put more thought into the way things sound when you say them, or more thought into the heart of respect behind the words you say?

   _____

   _____

   _____

   _____

2. In which relationships do you find it easy to practice respectful communication?

   _____

   _____

   _____

   _____

3. Why do you think that is?

   _____

   _____

   _____

   _____

4. What do you believe about the inherent value of people that sets your vision for how you treat them and are willing to be treated?

   _____

   _____

   _____

   _____

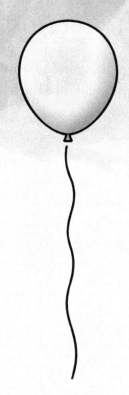

Day 64 – Openness

LIVING FROM
THE SPIRIT OF LOVE

*"A sound mind in a sound body, is a short, but full description
of a happy state in this World: he that has these two, has little more
to wish for; and he that wants either of them,
will be little the better for anything else."*

John Locke

"For God has not given us a spirit of fear but of power and of love and of a sound mind."

2 Timothy 1:7 NKJV

Have you noticed that Jesus didn't take all twelve of His disciples everywhere? All of His disciples were part of His inner circle, and specifically chosen by Him. But on at least three occasions, Peter, James, and John got to go with Jesus and see things the others weren't permitted to see. The most striking of these is the transfiguration. These three men got to see Jesus transfigured, His identity as the Son of God revealed to them in a deeper way. Jesus asks them not to speak of this until after His resurrection. We don't know why, but we know Jesus must have had a reason in line with His priorities. He didn't feel unhealthy fear or guilt for not "including" others. What we do know is that Jesus partnered with the spirit of love and wasn't afraid to make hard decisions and set limits in line with priorities.

God put in you a vibrant and strong spirit! This is the truth on days you feel it, and on days you don't feel it. Partnering with the spirit of love requires us to take full ownership of our words and actions, so that they communicate this love. Have you considered that the spirit of love is also God with a sound mind? The opposite, the spirit of fear, is the divided mind? A divided mind goes back and forth, struggling with decisions. A sound mind is confident in its choices. When we're setting boundaries, we have a choice to partner with the spirit of fear or the spirit of love. When we partner with the spirit of love, we think with a sound mind and we make responsible decisions. These decisions line our lives up with our priorities and protect our relationships.

Setting new boundaries in your relationships takes courage! If you find it daunting to make changes, or are worried about what people might think or say, you're not alone. Remember 1 John 4:18: "Perfect love casts out fear." As long as you are making decisions and communicating them from a place of love, if others do not like the decisions, you can allow them to deal with that in the way they need to, without taking on unhealthy guilt or shame. When we keep in mind what we have to gain, the temporary fear is easier to overcome in the name of love. Remember this verse from 2 Timothy 1:7: "For God hasn't given us a spirit of fear but of power and of love and of a sound mind!" The spirit within you knows how to overcome fear and operate out of love and a sound mind! Start by identifying what you're afraid of when it comes to setting boundaries, and choose instead to partner with the spirit of love.

Prayer

God, thank You for giving me everything I need
to make healthy and helpful decisions in my life.
Where I have let a spirit of fear govern my mind,
I now choose to surrender to the spirit You have given me—
one of love, power, and a sound mind.
Instruct me in the way of the Lord.
I want to live my life the way You would want me to.
Your spirit of love is the best thing that humanity has ever experienced.
Show me how to continue to live the way You live, Jesus.

Reflection

1. When it comes to setting boundaries, what are you most afraid of?

    _____

    _____

    _____

    _____

2. If your fear in this area was displaced by love, power, and a sound mind, what are some possible outcomes?

    _____

    _____

    _____

    _____

3. When it comes to making decisions in general, what causes you to become indecisive?

    _____

    _____

    _____

    _____

4. Write out a few lines that describe your commitment to let go of fear and ungodly guilt when setting boundaries and making decisions.

    _____

    _____

    _____

    _____

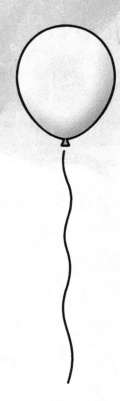

Day 65— Ownership

WATCHING OVER THE WORDS WE OWN

"Response-ability is the ABILITY to choose our response to any circumstance or condition."

Stephen Covey

"So then, my beloved brethren, let every man be swift to hear, slow to speak, slow to wrath; for the wrath of man does not produce the righteousness of God."

James 1:19-20 NKJV

Learning to be owners of our communication requires us to bring a high level of intentionality to our conversations. Just like all of us have the choice to take care of things we own like our homes, cars, and clothes, we have a choice to take ownership and care for our words. If you take pride in the car you own, you watch over it, use it carefully, and keep it clean and running smoothly so it helps get you where you want to go. If you take pride in your words, you will do the same. If you do not take pride in your things and your words, the opposite happens: your lack of care degrades and devalues the worth of what you own and what you say. When you stop caring for your car, your car stops working to get you where you want to go and instead becomes a source of increased frustration.

When we do not care for what we own, it actually impacts our sense of worth and value because we are not living according to God's perfect and divine plan. He called us to be stewards and if we are not stewarding well, our spirit feels it. That uncomfortable feeling is meant to motivate us to get back on track, but too often, we take our discomfort out on whomever is around us and react or blame them for it. Frustration, miscommunication, and harsh outbursts are all signs to tell us we can fine-tune our stewardship of our emotions, heart, and words. Reactionary words often come from a defensive stance, when we think we need to convince, manipulate, or pressure others into hearing us and responding to our needs. What we usually need most is to make sure we are hearing ourselves, and come up with a plan to get our needs met, regardless of what others do.

As a therapist, Ally spent many years learning the art of stewarding her words. This involves pausing and asking questions of yourself before bringing words into a conversation. Ally learned that instead of asking herself, "Is it good or right to say this to a client right now?" she would ask herself, "Is this helpful to say right now?" Speaking according to the latter always produced more fruitful, meaningful conversation. Ephesians 4:29 says our words should benefit those who hear them. James 1:19 reminds us to be quick to listen, slow to speak, and slow to anger. The best place to start to practice is with ourselves. When we have a thought about ourselves, it is important to ask if it is helpful to us. If it is producing bad fruit in us or in our relationships, that is a sign that we need to steward the garden of our heart and pull that weed out! We need to take care and pride in the words we use to describe ourselves and our worth. As we do, we will speak words to others that are fruit produced from a garden of value and worth, and we will be more helpful.

Prayer

God, thank You that one of the fruits of Your Spirit is self-control.
In times of conflict, I know that to react impulsively seldom has a good result.
I choose instead to prioritize connection and to learn ways to steward
my words and my emotions, so they better serve me.
Thank You that as I do this, I grow strong bonds in my relationships.
I can speak the truth in love and respond with care and compassion
while being strong in who I am in You and what I stand for.
Thank You, Jesus, that You are the best communicator.
You speak the words of life!

Reflection

1. What thoughts come to mind when you hear the word, "confrontation?"

   _____

   _____

   _____

   _____

2. Looking back over what you wrote, which thoughts or mindsets do not align with the person God has called you to be?

   _____

   _____

   _____

   _____

3. How might you surrender your natural thoughts for the Mind of Christ when it comes to confrontation?

   _____

   _____

   _____

   _____

4. How might you take care of yourself and build your sense of safety, to increase the likelihood of you responding instead of reacting?

   _____

   _____

   _____

   _____

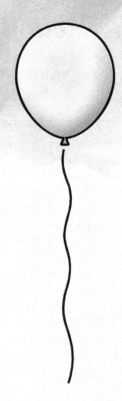

Day 66~ Openness

LIVING FROM THE COVENANT OF GRACE

"For grace is given not because we have done good works, but in order that we may be able to do them."

Saint Augustine of Hippo

"Brothers and sisters, if someone is caught in a sin, you who live by the Spirit should restore that person gently."

Galatians 6:1 NIV

The foundation that sustains life is grace. It's not some "path of least resistance," "get out of jail free card." With grace, our body lives, we breath, and things work. When the grace runs up, movement ceases. The great invitation inside of grace is that people are brought up into the restoration of Christ. This is incredible for everyone! The standard we get to receive is not by our merits, our sins, our faults; it's by Him! Our perfect Savior Jesus. We receive His sufficient grace for our lives. This gives us life, meaning, purpose, and power!

The divine tension that must be held is knowing and adopting this great grace from Jesus while still abiding responsibly in His attitudes. His grace should change us to become more like Him. We should be attracted to His attributes and thus mimic His thoughts, behavior, and life. As we receive this great grace freely, we should also understand there is a price that must be paid. It costs a great deal to cleanse the sin of a person and restore them to their better self with forgiveness. We carry the burden of the sin or we allow it to be carried by God. Let's give our burden to the Lord and receive His grace in exchange.

Galatians 6:1 says, "Brothers and sisters, if someone is caught in a sin, you who live by the Spirit should restore that person gently." When God looks at us, He's always thinking about how to restore and heal our broken places into wholeness, and we need to look with this lens too when we face our own, or others', mistakes and sin. Ephesians 4:32 says, "Be kind and compassionate to one another, forgiving each other, just as in Christ God forgave you." Now, it's supernatural that you and I would have the power to forgive someone, because forgiveness comes from God. If we believe that we have the power to forgive, we also have the power to restore grace back to someone who fell short in our lives.

Prayer

God, thank You for Your Grace that strengthens and brings life to my body, mind, and soul. Your yoke is easy and Your burden is so light in the presence of what seems to be such a heavy burden that I carry. I will give it to You. Lord, help me to realize Your grace today and hold it in holy reverence because the life you give me is because of the price You paid. Thank You so much! I love You, Jesus.

Reflection

1. What comes up in your heart and mind when you think of the word "grace"?

   _____

   _____

   _____

   _____

2. How can you apply more grace in your relationships?

   _____

   _____

   _____

   _____

3. When someone lets you down or falls short, how can you restore them gently?

   _____

   _____

   _____

   _____

4. Try to remember the last time you disappointed yourself. How might you change your approach and start empowering yourself into change?

   _____

   _____

   _____

   _____

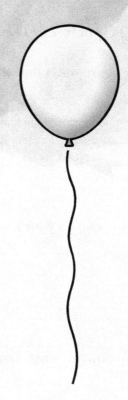

Day 67 – Ownership

OUR MISSION IS
TO LEARN TO LOVE

*"True friends don't spend time gazing into each other's eyes.
They may show great tenderness toward each other but they face
in the same direction—toward common projects,
goals—above all, toward a common Lord."*

C. S. Lewis

*"And now these three remain: faith, hope and love.
But the greatest of these is love."*

1 Corinthians 13:13 NIV

Each one of us was created by God for a purpose, and our calling is part of this purpose. Some of us are clear on what our purpose and calling is, and others are still figuring it out with God. For all of us though, our biggest calling will always really just be about the people we're called to love and be in a relationship with. One of the most heartbreaking things we have seen are leaders who ran after a "calling" and in doing so, neglected their families and relationships. We often think of a story about a man named Bob Jones. He died and when he got to heaven, the question he was asked was not about how much money he raised or souls he led to salvation. Instead, the only question asked of him was, "Did you learn to love?"

The depth of relationships we have with others and the depth of love we give is what we will be measured by. Not the influence we had, or the number of people we reached. It is quality, not quantity, in the kingdom. Jesus could have had hundreds of thousands of disciples, but instead He chose twelve, and of those, had an especially close relationship with only three! He chose quality over quantity, and pouring in love to those twelve through simple conversations and "boring" everyday activities was how He operated.

Jesus warned us that people would say, "Didn't I prophesy? Didn't I do amazing things in your name?" (Matthew 7:22). And yet we are told it means nothing if we're not in a relationship with Jesus. Loving relationships are Jesus's highest priority. As we discover our mission, we must stay connected to the fact that our ultimate mission is not the things we do; it is if we do them from a place of love. Love does not mean we own the moods, emotions, or problems of others. It does not mean we allow people to do whatever they want when it hurts us or others. It does mean we do our best to own the moods, emotions, and problems that are ours, so that we can leave others better than we found them. Jesus's whole mission was to demonstrate love to the world in action and words. We believe that when we follow God's commandments to love each other really well as our top priority, we start to experience a taste of heaven on earth.

Prayer

God, I know that the work You have given me to do
depends on my ability to navigate relationships in a healthy way.
As I pursue a vision for my identity and calling, I choose to continue on the course
You have set for me with determination, even through the difficult seasons.
Teach me to apply the principles of healthy communication,
and by doing so, demonstrate my love for others.
I desire to know and fully engage in my mission to learn to love.
I know that to fully choose You is also to choose to align myself
with Your vision of love for others.

Reflection

1. How have strong friendships helped you to achieve your mission either personally or professionally?

    _____

    _____

    _____

    _____

2. Who in your life have you come alongside, encouraged, and championed in their mission? How did it feel?

    _____

    _____

    _____

    _____

3. If you were asked, "Did you learn to love" today, what would your honest response be?

    _____

    _____

    _____

    _____

4. Is there anything that comes to mind that you might need to change in order to be more open to shifting your mission to be one of learning to love?

    _____

    _____

    _____

    _____

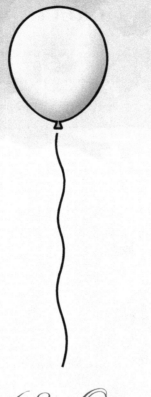

Day 68 ~ Openness

POURING OUT LOVE

"The giving of love is an education in itself."

Eleanor Roosevelt

"Be completely humble and gentle; be patient, bearing with one another in love. Make every effort to keep the unity of the Spirit through the bond of peace."

Ephesians 4:2-3 NIV

ommunication is about much more than just what we say. We're communicating with each other all the time, in the things we do, the things we don't do, the choices we make, and countless other ways. You can use all the communication tools in the world when there's conflict, but research shows that the little things you do each day make a bigger relational difference than the big things you do once in a while. Ephesians 4:2-3 encourages us to treat each other "with all humility and gentleness, with patience, bearing with one another in love, eager to maintain the unity of the Spirit in the bond of peace" (ESV). When we carry an awareness of this, it impacts our daily choices.

In his book The 5 Love Languages, Gary Chapman uses the helpful analogy of "love tanks" to explain how our daily choices to love impact the strength of our connections with others. Imagine we each have a "love tank" in our hearts. Every time we have a positive experience of love, our tank fills up. Every time we have a negative experience of love, the tank is drained. If we fill more than we drain, we're able to weather negative experiences from a place of fullness and security. If our love tank is constantly being drained and never filled, we have no resources to face negative experiences when they come. The strength of our relational connection depends on our daily choice to fill the other person's love tank. We fill someone's love tanks with our daily decision to love them in ways that are meaningful to them. This could look like taking time to ask about their day, giving surprise gifts, sending messages, or showing physical affection. Keeping each other's love tanks full is the best way to keep our connection strong!

Isn't it amazing that Jesus knows how to love each one of us individually? As we draw close in relationship with Him, He finds ways to communicate with us and love us that are different from anybody else. We all have unique needs, and receive love in different ways, but He knows all these things that make us unique. Part of the joy of loving another person is getting to discover their uniqueness, and how to reach their heart with love. There is nothing better than being loved by somebody who has taken the time to truly know you. As we make the daily choice to fill up each other's love tanks, we're making the choice to love others as Jesus loves us. Start by choosing somebody today whom you'd like to love better. Spend a week being intentional about filling up their love tank, and watch what happens!

Prayer

Thank You, Jesus, for loving me uniquely.
I'm so grateful that You know my innermost thoughts, pursue my heart,
and continuously fill my life with Your love in ways that are meaningful to me.
I choose to love others as You have loved me, taking the time to know them and love them
in meaningful ways. I choose to intentionally fill the love tanks of those close to me
with my daily decisions, so that we can build strong, unbreakable bonds of love.

Reflection

1. How full does your love tank feel on most days?

    _____

    _____

    _____

    _____

2. Whom might you communicate your needs to when it is
    feeling empty? What can you ask for specifically?

    _____

    _____

    _____

    _____

3. Do you find you have more patience, grace, and connection
    in relationships when the other person is actively filling
    your love tank?

    _____

    _____

    _____

    _____

4. In what ways can you fill up the love tanks of people closest to you?
    Be creative and write down a list of things you might try.

    _____

    _____

    _____

    _____

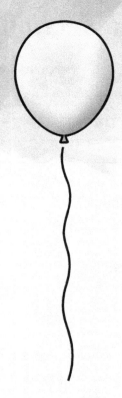

Day 69 – Ownership

THE POWER OF COMMITMENTS

Commitment fuels vision and vision fuels commitment.
Neither will produce without the other.

Brian Houston

People who are owners of their life keep their commitments to each other, and they trust themselves to make commitments they can keep. This sounds easy enough, but it can take a little practice. Boundaries are only effective if we follow through with them. Have you ever seen what happens when you try to discipline a child with empty threats? They quickly learn that you don't mean what you say. Redirecting your relationships in line with your priorities often starts with making new choices, setting new boundaries, and sticking to them until they become habits. Matthew 5:37 says, "Let what you say simply be 'Yes' and 'No.'" When we get really good at this, we'll not only see others start to trust us to mean what we say, but we'll build trust with ourselves as well.

Setting boundaries is about protecting your priorities. When you say "yes" to something, you're saying "no" to a whole bunch of other things, possibly really good things! At first, everything you've said no to might pop into your mind, or you might doubt yourself or feel guilty. But if you consistently set a firm boundary around your "yes," eventually the things you said no to will stop being viable options in your mind. It will become a lifestyle to live within your boundaries, and a joy to protect your priorities with your "yes!"

Jesus lived His life protecting His priority of connection to the Father. This meant He needed time alone, time to pray, time just with Him and

His disciples, time to eat and sleep and look after His health. Imagine the need that surrounded Him, the people who wanted His attention or were hoping for a miracle. Luke 5:16 tells us that Jesus "frequently withdrew to the lonely places to pray." This likely meant saying "no" to a crowd and even to His disciples, but He consistently kept this commitment to Himself. Because of this, He was able to keep His commitments to others and build trust with others.

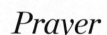

Prayer

God, thank You for Your commitment to me.
Thank You for the security that is available in relationships
built on the foundation of trust. I choose to be someone
who is faithful in my commitments to others,
and to become brilliant at communicating what I will and won't do
so that my words carry weight and build trust.
You are true and faithful in Your commitments to me, Jesus,
and I will extend the same forthright actions to my relationships.
You are my guide and my leader.

Reflection

1. Do you struggle with guilt when you say, "No"? If so, where is that guilt coming from?

    _____

    _____

    _____

    _____

2. Do you find yourself avoiding saying "no" to people, or committing to things and not following through?

    _____

    _____

    _____

    _____

3. Consider God's commitment to you; how does it make you feel to know He is 100% committed to you?

    _____

    _____

    _____

    _____

4. How might you best demonstrate your commitment to God and the life He has called you to live today?

    _____

    _____

    _____

    _____

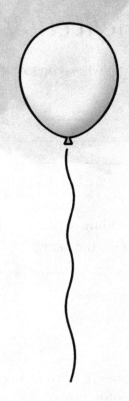

Day 70– Openness

GOD'S PROMISE TO US

*"Some people still make promises and keep those they make.
When they do, they help make life around them more stably human."*

Lewis B. Smedes

"For all the promises of God in Him are Yes, and in Him Amen, to the glory of God through us."

2 Corinthians 1:20 NKJV

Did you know scholars can find more than 3000 promises from God to us in the Bible? God isn't afraid of promises, and as believers we know that promises are His unchangeable commitment to us. He makes promises to us because He is confident of His ability to fulfill them, and when we trust Him we're saying we are confident in His ability too. In short, He takes ownership to fulfill His promises, no matter what we do or don't do. 2 Corinthians 1:20 tells us, "For all the promises of God in Him are Yes, and in Him 'Amen, to the glory of God through us." This means that we can trust what He says is true, and what He's promised will be fulfilled, including His promises to us about our relationships.

God is faithful to deliver on His promises, even when it looks different than what we were expecting or takes longer than we think. When God promised Abraham a son, both he and Sarah were old. They trusted and waited but she didn't become pregnant. Eventually, Sarah brought Abraham her servant, and he conceived a child with her, instead. That child, though, wasn't the promise, and nothing Sarah and Abraham did could stop Him fulfilling His promise to them. In time, Sarah became pregnant with Isaac, who was the fulfilment of the promise. God's faithfulness to own His promise is greater than our capacity to believe Him, and greater than our actions and our mistakes. We should partner with boundaries and not allow any of our choices to keep us from walking into the fullness of the promises of God. The Israelites wandered in the

Wilderness for forty years before getting their promise because they did not set boundaries with doubt in their minds and hearts.

As we trust and as He fulfills, it brings us deeper connection. It shows us that He means what He says. But the opposite is also true; when we do not keep our promises, we injure ourselves and our relationships very deeply—sometimes, past the point of repair. Promises demonstrate boundaries with anything that might try to separate us from love. This is why a husband and wife make promises during their wedding, verbalizing their willingness to set boundaries with anything that might try to get in the way of the relationship. God not only keeps His promises to you, but He can empower you to keep your promises to others. As you take hold of your promises and walk toward them, trust God to fulfil His promise of bringing peace to you. Trust Him today to lead you into healthy, happy relationships.

Prayer

God, thank You that it says in Your word that all the promises of God are yes and amen.
We know You as a loving Father, faithful to fulfill the promises over our lives,
including those concerning relationships.
I choose to focus on Your promises and live in faith to see Your promises
fulfilled in my life. You have set in the Heavens thousands of promises for us.
We love You for this! Every one of Your promises are good and they are for my benefit.
Teach me to delight in Your promises each and every day.

Reflection

1. Describe a testimony of God's promise being fulfilled in your life or the life of someone you love.

    _____

    _____

    _____

    _____

2. Are there any promises that God has given you that you might have given up on too soon?

    _____

    _____

    _____

    _____

3. What is one promise God has spoken over you that reveals His heart toward you?

    _____

    _____

    _____

    _____

4. How would being careful to keep your promises impact your relationships for the better?

    _____

    _____

    _____

    _____

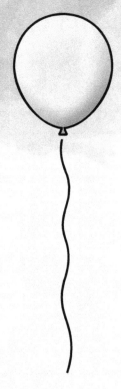

Day 71 – Ownership

LOVE
IN ACTION

"Our culture says that feelings of love are the basis for actions of love. And of course, that can be true. But it is truer to say that actions of love can lead consistently to feelings of love."

Timothy Keller

"My little children, let us not love in word or in tongue, but in deed and in truth."

1 John 3:18 NKJV

Love is more than just a warm, fuzzy feeling or an emotion; it's the act of walking out the message "I choose you." We all have different love languages, but each love language is connected to an action, something you do to communicate that love, or something you need in order to receive it. Setting boundaries is another important way to attach action to your feelings. It backs up the message "I love you" with proof that we're willing to sacrifice other things to protect and nourish the love we feel in our hearts and confess with our lips. 1 John 3:18 says, "My little children, let us not love in word or in tongue, but in deed and in truth." This tells us that while our words are important, love is tested in our actions.

Setting boundaries is about being consistent in telling ourselves what to do and following through on our choices. It's also about getting good at telling others what we will and won't do. When we think about boundaries, we often think about the people we're saying "no" to, but it is just as important to think about the feelings of the person we're saying "yes" to. It is important to communicate "no" without excuses. It is also important to know that we can say no even while having compassion for others and deeply caring about them. For example, one might say no to a request for a call from a person seeking help with their car, if they want to spend more time with their family that evening. If we orient ourselves around those that have the biggest need, we often neglect those we are called to love even when there is no deep, gaping need. If we only respond to the biggest need, we do not actually own our life; the biggest need owns our life, and we fail to be intentional about what matters to us, and the relationships God gave us.

If we tell our spouse we love them, but always interrupt conversations with them to take calls from people who call us to vent about a bad day, the words, "I love you," "I value you" cease to have meaning to our spouse. Jesus told us the poor will always be with us. There are people who are emotionally and spiritually poor all the time, but that is no reason to neglect those closest to us, and neglect to spend our time and resources with them. If we want people to believe the feeling we have and the words we speak, we must demonstrate this by making them a priority in our lives. This starts by becoming comfortable saying "no" to others, reinforcing that we should not drop everything to take ownership of others' lives. When you demonstrate this commitment guilt-free, you'll build strong bonds of trust where they matter most.

Prayer

God, thank You for every new revelation You've given me in love.
I choose to translate these into actions so that Your transformative power can
begin to work in my relationships. Thank You for revealing the right first step
for me, right now. Where can I act today? How can I put love into action?
Speak to me words of instruction at night; seal them up in my heart.
Share love notes with me during the day or when I am praying with You.
I want to put Your love in motion with each and every person
You have given me. Thank You for Your love.

Reflection

1. How do you start to feel when you see someone's actions
   don't line up with the values they claim to have?
   How does it erode connection?

   _____

   _____

   _____

   _____

2. Where might you need to set boundaries to protect your "yes"?

   _____

   _____

   _____

   _____

3. Do you find yourself trying to make excuses for saying "no"?

   _____

   _____

   _____

   _____

4. Where could you demonstrate your love with an action this week?

   _____

   _____

   _____

   _____

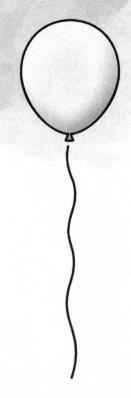

NEW RELATIONAL TOOLS

"Good relationships require a lot of hard work, education, and willingness to meet each other's needs."

Joyce Meyer

"Now may the God of peace, who through the blood of the eternal covenant brought back from the dead our Lord, Jesus, that great Shepherd of the sheep, equip you with everything good for doing His will, and may He work in us what is pleasing to Him, through Jesus Christ, to whom be glory for ever and ever. Amen."

Hebrews 13:20-21 NIV

Some of us grew up in a healthy relational environment, and inherited great relational tools. If this is you, you probably don't think much about how the tools work; they're instinctive and positive results usually "just happen." For others of us, we inherited tools that do the opposite. We might be more aware in this case of what's not working, but often our willpower isn't enough to change the pattern. Often, when we can't change patterns, it is because we are trying to use a manipulative control on ourselves, instead of cultivating a loving and empowering relationship with ourselves that has healthy boundaries.

We have heard so many people try to change bad habits by changing their behavior first. They try hard to stop yelling, stop overeating, and stop being late. The problem is, these behaviors are just symptoms of a bigger problem. Usually, that problem is a lack of love, respect, and value for oneself. When we do something we do not like and punish ourselves with shame and guilt, we only perpetuate the cycle. We focus on what is wrong instead of focusing our time and energy on taking ownership to discover what DOES work. We can't just focus on what we "won't" do; we also need to find healthy tools to replace the ones that don't work. Many of us have made promises that we will "never be like our parents," but the minute we find ourselves in a painful or scary situation, we find ourselves saying the exact thing we've heard a hundred times before and using the same manipulative tools. As we go on the journey of discovering new tools, and move from control to self-control, we discover new tools that create loving connections.

Transforming our lives and relationships means identifying the best tools for doing relationships well. Even if you've never thought about it this way, we're all already using tools in relationships. The question is, are these tools working for you? Where did you learn them? Hebrews promises us that Jesus equips us with everything good for doing His will (Hebrews 13:20-21). It's definitely His will that we have healthy relationships with each other, so it's our job to identify which of our tools are working well, and which need replacing with new ones!

Prayer

God, You are my ever-present help.
I recognize the times I have felt powerless,
and ask You to show me the power Jesus died to give me in each situation.
Open my eyes to where I have been blind to see the redemptive plan You have
for any lack in my relational tool set. In the relational challenges I face,
You have not left me stranded or abandoned without a way forward.
I worship You as the creator and provider of all good tools!
Your Word is full of practical information and tools for growing and expanding
in my capacity to bear good fruit. Where I have opportunities for growth,
highlight the right tools and resources to me so that I can live my life
in a way that glorifies You.

Reflection

. How have the relational tools you inherited from your family environment helped you thrive in your adult life?

_____

_____

_____

_____

2. How have the relational tools you inherited from your family held you back in your adult life?

_____

_____

_____

_____

3. Which relational tools are working for you in your current relationships?

_____

_____

_____

_____

4. For the tools you might like to gain or replace, who is a model you might look at to demonstrate other options for behavior?

_____

_____

_____

_____

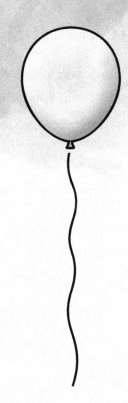

Day 73– Ownership

PROTECTING YOUR RELATIONSHIP WITH GOD

*"Exploring the desire of our hearts is not a waste of time.
It is precisely the place where God is stirring. It is the golden cord
of our connection to God and to each other."*

Paula Rinehart

"Delight yourself also in the Lord,
and He shall give you the desires of your heart. "

Psalm 37:4 NKJV

We are all born with an innate desire for God, and this desire can't be fulfilled through any human relationship. The innermost circle of your heart is your core. Some people call this the "God spot," because He's the only person who belongs in the core of your heart and spirit. Nobody will ever know you like Jesus, and nobody else deserves your heart's worship. The Bible tells us, "Delight yourself also in the Lord, and He shall give you the desires of your heart." Psalm 37:4 tells us that when we set our desire first on the Lord, He is also faithful to fulfill our other desires, too. Isn't it interesting that the Psalm tells us that when we do this one thing, the other things fall into place?

In Matthew 22:36, one of the Sadducees asks Jesus, "Which is the greatest commandment in the law?" Jesus replies, "'Love the Lord your God with all your heart and all your soul and all your mind.' This is the first and greatest commandment, and the second is like it: 'Love your neighbor as you love yourself'" (Matthew 22:37-40). In this verse Jesus is demonstrating this same progression. First love God with everything in you, and from that place you'll be able to love yourself and others. He is revealing the core truth about how to live our best lives, because He knows what we need! This is why He only did what the Father was doing. He was keeping God in His "God spot," knowing that this would enable Him to love others well.

What boundaries might we want to set to protect our connection with God? When our first big "yes" is to God, our other relationships thrive too. We were created in the image of a relational God, which means that we are relational by design. This verse tells us that this design has an order and a priority to it. Our most important relationship is with Him, the one who created us. In this relationship we receive everything we most need: identity, security, belonging, and purpose. Getting this relationship right is the key to getting our relationships with ourselves and others right. In fact, one of the signs that God is in the "God spot" is that our other relationships are thriving!

Prayer

God, thank You for placing Your desires in my heart.
Where I desire healthy and committed relationships, I thank You
that You have already set the course necessary to see this desire fulfilled.
I choose to delight in You, and to partner with what You're saying and doing in my life.
I want to protect my connection with You at all costs. You alone
have first place in my heart. Bring forth Your spirit and grace to fill me up
with Your love so I may be overwhelmed with Your embrace.
I want to be near You all the days of my life. Send forth guardian angels
to protect the connection that we have.
Thank You so much, Jesus.

Reflection

1. Do you feel fully known and loved by God?

   _____

   _____

   _____

   _____

2. If not, what do you feel like you are hiding from Him?
   What do you fear He does not like or appreciate about you?

   _____

   _____

   _____

   _____

3. What scriptures might you use to help calm your fears and feelings
   you need to be in hiding?

   _____

   _____

   _____

   _____

4. How might you "delight yourself also in the Lord" today?

   _____

   _____

   _____

   _____

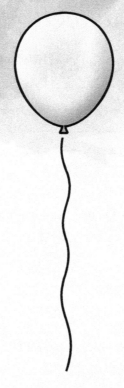

Day 74~ Openness

SEEKING
GOD'S WISDOM

"We cannot solve our problems with the same thinking we used
when we created them."

Albert Einstein

"Blessed are those who find Wisdom and those who gain understanding."

Proverbs 3:13 NIV

*I*n Acts 6, we see the early church multiplying and growing. Word was getting out and the number of disciples were increasing, as were the number of people who came for healing or to be looked after. At this time, "a complaint arose on the part of the Hellenistic Jews against the native Hebrews, because their widows were being overlooked in the daily serving of food" (Acts 6:1). So the twelve gathered together and came up with a solution. They needed to protect their time for ministry, so they appointed other leaders to manage the distribution of food. The Bible tells us that after this, the word spread rapidly! Needing to think, reassess, and make new plans is a natural part of life.

God made you to rule and reign, which means He must trust you to make judgments and decisions, to discern right from wrong and to operate out of wisdom. He also knows that He is with you and His spirit is a brilliant inspiration when you're stuck. To become more like Jesus is a choice we make, empowered by the Holy Spirit. It requires us to think about our thoughts and actions and choose to make necessary changes. Proverbs 3:13 says, "Blessed are those who find Wisdom and those who gain understanding." Wisdom and understanding are available to us when we seek them out.

People who take ownership are not afraid to find what's not working and look for wisdom for a new plan! We all have "autopilots," and when these are set to great destinations, there's no need to change them. But, if they are not, we need to think about our reactions until we can reprogram them to go where we want to go. Most of us do not intentionally plan to listen to fear and let that be more important than love. But when that happens, in order to get connected again, we will need to find our inner resources to think, choose, and act in a way that will bring change. Powerless people say, "This keeps happening to me! Things will never change!" People who have a sense of ownership respond with, "That didn't work, but I can think about it and choose differently in the future to get a different result." You can choose your future, choose to keep connection, and choose to keep working toward relational unity!

Prayer

God, You designed my mind!
You gave me the ability to think, to solve problems, and to grapple with ideas.
Thank You that You have given me the mind of Christ,
so that I would have access to heavenly wisdom.
Expand my vision to see solutions where I used to see problems.
As Elisha's eyes were opened to see Your invisible army,
let me see the invisible forces working together for my good,
and Your vision of my solution when I am in crisis!
Where I have doubted my ability to think, I repent.
I understand that developing good discernment can take time and practice,
and I am committed to taking the journey of growth
with You by my side!

Reflection

1. What is one thing that is not working as well as you would like it to be right now?

    _____
    _____
    _____
    _____

2. Spend a few minutes pursuing wisdom on the topic.
    Talk to friends, read the Bible, do some research.

    _____
    _____
    _____
    _____

3. Identify one step you can take toward change in a positive direction and commit to take that action.

    _____
    _____
    _____
    _____

4. What actions and words might you choose that demonstrate your love, even if you do not immediately find the perfect solution?

    _____
    _____
    _____
    _____

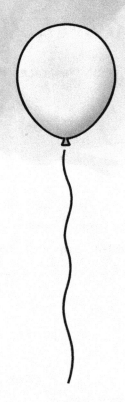

Day 75— Ownership

OWNING
FORGIVENESS

"Forgiveness is the giving, and so the receiving, of life."

George MacDonald

"Get rid of all bitterness, rage and anger, brawling and slander, along with every form of malice. Be kind to one another, tenderhearted, forgiving one another, as God in Christ forgave you."

Ephesians 4:31-32

In Matthew 18:27-35, Jesus tells us the story of a servant and his master. The servant owed the master a great sum of money, but the master let him off the hook and cancelled his debt. The servant then went to another servant who owed him a lesser debt. Instead of cancelling the debt as his master had done, the servant had the man thrown into prison. When the master heard about this, he called the servant back. "You wicked servant," he said. "I cancelled your debt. Shouldn't you have had mercy on your fellow servant just as I had on you?" In anger, the master handed him over to the jailers to be tortured until he could pay back what he owed. Unforgiveness tortures us, because we don't have the power to cause anyone else to forgive. When we choose unforgiveness, we are opening the door for harsher self-judgment in our own mind, and choosing to give others power we should take ownership of. God wants to protect us from that destruction.

Sometimes forgiveness feels easy in the moment, and sometimes it's a choice we make day after day until the feeling catches up with our decision. Hard as it might be sometimes, forgiveness is an essential part of our healing and restoration, whether we're asking for forgiveness or offering it. When Jesus died for us on the cross, He forgave us everything, without question! It was not good for Him to continue to bear the burden of all the bad we did; He left it when He died on the cross. Unforgiveness is like someone else leaving junk in your yard, and instead of throwing it in the trash or bringing it back to its owner, you bag it up and carry it around with you wherever you go, waiting for it to come back to you and claim it. What a waste of time and energy! Ephesians 4:31-32 tells us, "Get rid of all bitterness, rage and anger, brawling and slander, along with every form of malice. Be kind to one another, tenderhearted, forgiving one another, as God in Christ forgave you."

God knows that unforgiveness is toxic to our hearts, and affects how we love and interact with our communities, and even with Him. Unforgiveness ties us to wrongs, and causes us to feel a false sense of ownership for the wrong, and for righting a wrong we did not commit. We often think that we need to get somebody to repent, apologize, or prove they have changed before we offer them forgiveness. That is not our job. Forgiveness is our job, regardless of what the other person does or doesn't do. Jesus allows us to exchange the hurt for forgiveness that frees us. When we choose to forgive people from our heart, it doesn't mean we have to trust them again or let them back into our life. It does not mean we accept their behavior. It does mean that we are able to love, implement boundaries, and refuse to allow their bad choices to be the owner of how we act in life. When we choose forgiveness, for ourselves and others, we choose to align ourselves with God's kingdom and all our relationships reap the benefit.

✦

Prayer

God, I enter into Your love knowing I am fully forgiven.
I am aware I am not bound by any mistake or wrong I have done,
but I am bound by Your love. I know that Your love covers sins, and holding on
to unforgiveness toward others drives a wedge between me and Your love.
Today, I choose to release, let go, and forgive those who have wronged and hurt me.
I choose only to have the burden of receiving Your love and healing where I need it.
I choose to hope for restoration instead of destruction,
just as You did for me.

Reflection

. What damage have you seen unforgiveness cause on people
who do not forgive?

_____

_____

_____

_____

2. When have you felt the joy of God's forgiveness the most?

_____

_____

_____

_____

3. Is there a testimony or story of forgiveness that has inspired you?
Why? What happened that impacted you about forgiveness?

_____

_____

_____

_____

4. Are there any obstacles to accepting God's love and forgiveness
for yourself?

_____

_____

_____

_____

Day 76– Openness

RESPONDING
TO MISTAKES

*"Failure happens all the time. It happens every day in practice.
What makes you better is how you react to it."*

Mia Hamm

"Though he may stumble, he will not fall, for the Lord upholds him with His hand."

Psalm 37:24 NIV

You might be afraid of your mistakes, but God is not afraid of them at all! When we learn to set good boundaries and protect our relationships, mistakes become part of the process of learning to love well, rather than something to be feared. The Gospel message is: "I love you no matter what." And with love, we can walk out the consequences of mistakes to turn them into positive stepping stones on our journey. God knows how to redeem every situation and turn it around for your good! When we understand this, we realize there is no need to fear our mistakes, or the mistakes of others. Psalm 37:24 says, "Though he may stumble, he will not fall, for the Lord upholds him with His hand." The Lord has your back in the midst of your mistakes!

We can't deny that mistakes happen. Our mistakes and the mistakes of others affect our lives to varying degrees, but that doesn't mean we have to be afraid of them. Instead, we can choose how we respond to our mistakes and the mistakes of others. Will we respond with love, or will we respond in fear? Too often, fear is the first response to mistakes, and fear leads to control. If we respond with love instead, we resist power and control and choose to come alongside the person who made the mistake, find the root issue that leads to the mistake, and offer strength to them as they clean up their mess and come into a place of restoration. Mistakes can be messy and scary, but God is not afraid of them and we shouldn't be either . In every mistake, He sees an opportunity to lead His sons and daughters into a greater revelation of who they truly are.

Our relationships bring us through our trials and mistakes better than anything else. It is those we bring around us that should call us up higher and hold our arms up in the midst of trying times. When we make mistakes in our relationships, there are relational processes that bring us back into alignment. Relational mistakes take relational mending, spiritual mistakes take spiritual mending, and so on... When we retrace the origin of how we have arrived at our mistake, it will help in the repair process. God will empower us as we retool, rebuild, and move forward. His clarity and grace will provide us the way.

Prayer

God, You sent Your Son so that I could live in freedom.
As I navigate growth in every area of my life, I choose to extend the same grace
to myself as You extend to me. Where fear of failure has kept me stuck, I remind myself
that there is no failure in You. Show me the way to have redemption in all of my areas
of lack and when I fall short. Hold my hand and lead me through the valley
of my mistakes. Show me where I can learn and how I should respond.
You are the best leader that is so compassionate and redemptive.
I glean from you. Thank You, Jesus.

Reflection

1. In which areas of life have you felt like you can't move forward because you're scared of getting things wrong?

_____

_____

_____

_____

2. How can you start to respond in love toward yourself instead of fear when you make a mistake?

_____

_____

_____

_____

3. Think of a recent mistake you made. How might your Father in heaven, who is perfect, love you through that mistake?

_____

_____

_____

_____

4. Remember and write about a time God used something people thought was a mistake to fulfill His plan.

_____

_____

_____

_____

Day 77 – Ownership

BOUNDARIES WITH YOUR INNER CIRCLE

"You know you are with true friends when they lift, encourage, correct, and then spur you on."

Lisa Bevere

321

Boundaries can be hardest with our closest friends. Have you ever felt that somebody close to you started to behave like a consumer, but you weren't sure how to set appropriate limits? We can worry about hurting their feelings, afraid that we're being selfish, or tell ourselves it's a difficult time that will pass. But the same principle applies to everybody: if we're not tending to our own garden and managing our resources, we need to adjust so we can keep loving, even if this means setting limits with those closest to us. Covenants aren't just for marriages; they're for close friendships, too. 1 Samuel 18:3 tells us, "Jonathan made a covenant with David because he loved him as himself." Just like within marriage, we protect our connection with our close friends when we know how to manage our own resources of love well.

We need to know how to set limits in our close relationships. This can be hard because these are the relationships that are closest to our heart. They have more access to our lives and our resources than others, but that doesn't mean they get to define what resources they have access to. We manage these relationships well when we remember that we get to control what we will and won't do. If a close friend expresses a need, we get to choose to meet it. If they keep expressing needs and expect them to be met without meeting our needs in return, or demand more from us than the access we've given, we will need to set a limit. If we don't, the relationship gets out of balance quickly and is likely to lead to feelings of resentment. The fruitfulness of our lives is dependent on our ability to set limits with even our best friends. While it might feel painful to say, "No," an appropriate "no" protects the relationship and builds stronger friendships. If the other person reacts negatively, maybe they were not as great friends as we thought.

Boundaries are a sign of health. It shows great care and consideration to set boundaries. The misconception is that boundaries are for someone else, like a friend or your family member. Boundaries are for you! You place the boundaries; you uphold them. It is an internal process to keep you healthy. At the end of the day, if you remove the other involved people from your life, you still have your boundaries. If you place a boundary around another person, that is called control. What does that mean, boundaries are for me and not for the other person? It means, boundaries are not an excuse to control someone else; they are an internal process to protect you.

✦

Prayer

God, thank You for being my best friend.
Thank You that Jesus demonstrated a healthy pattern for relationships
and prioritized some over others. I choose to prioritize the relationships in my life
according to levels of intimacy and to protect the spot only You can fill.
You are the master of good and life-giving boundaries.
I look to You to help me establish guard rails in my close relationships.
You have shown us through Your word that boundaries are good and life-giving.
Thank You, Jesus, for that. Guide me in the right direction.
Help me establish the best boundaries
that help me keep loving.

Reflection

1. Recall a time when you said yes to a close friend just to avoid hurting their feelings. If you could go back, what else could you have said to set a boundary with love?

   _____

   _____

   _____

   _____

2. What are the boundaries God would like for you to set with your close friends?

   _____

   _____

   _____

   _____

3. Are your close relationships a balance of give and take, or are they lopsided?

   _____

   _____

   _____

   _____

4. Are there any needs and desires only God can fulfill that you tend to try to get met by your close friends and family?

   _____

   _____

   _____

   _____

Day 78– Openness

WISDOM
IN CHOICES

*"In any moment of decision, the best thing you can do
is the right thing, the next best thing you can do is the wrong thing,
and the worst thing you can do is nothing."*

Theodore Roosevelt

An indicator of someone becoming an owner of their life is they're willingness to make choices about their lives and take responsibility for those choices. This doesn't mean they're always 100% sure of the choice, or that they're always right. It just means they're willing to step out of the powerless no man's land of indecision and move forward. When we're not sure what to do, we can pray for discernment with our choices. In Philippians 1:9, Paul prays that the Philippians would grow in knowledge and discernment. This tells us that with God's help, we can grow in our discernment with choices, too.

People who do not know how to take ownership often get stuck in indecision because of fear. They worry about whether they'll make the wrong decision, what other people will think, and if there will be unforeseen consequences. They may even worry about their own ability to stick to the decision once it's made. To choose is one of the most fulfilling and life-giving actions we can take. To choose means to accept responsibility for our lives and actions, to let go of what we can't control and embrace what we can: ourselves. Fear doesn't need to be part of our decision-making process! If we're living in the right relationship with God, we can trust that we have discernment to make great choices about our lives because the Holy Spirit lives in us.

We see an example of ownership for decisions in the book of Ruth. Naomi has two sons, who are married to Ruth and Orpah. After Naomi's husband and sons die, Naomi decides to return to her homeland. At first, Ruth and Orpah go with her, but Naomi stops and gives them a choice. She tells them to go back to the homes of their fathers and find new men to marry. The women protest, but eventually Orpah leaves them and does as Naomi has suggested. Ruth, on the other hand, is adamant that she will stay with Naomi. She is travelling to a foreign land, with foreign gods, leaving everything behind with little hope of marrying again. Her future is completely uncertain, and yet in that moment, she chooses the relationship with Naomi no matter what. Owners aren't afraid to make choices in line with their priorities, even if the outcome is uncertain. They know that no matter what happens, they have the power to course-correct later, if needed.

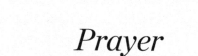

Prayer

*God, thank You that Your desire is for us to be discerning
as we make choices in relationship with You. Thank You that as I make choices
with a surrendered heart, You're able to direct my path and lead me in the way of life
and increase. I choose to look to You for the wisdom of the ages in my life.
You are my answer and my source for all wisdom and understanding.
I know I can depend on You to guide me and assist me in all of my choices.
I love Your assistance and welcome it
each and every day!*

Reflection

. Do you feel you or others should have to be 100% right before making a decision?

_____

_____

_____

_____

2. In the decisions you are currently facing, what are you afraid will happen if you are not 100% right?

_____

_____

_____

_____

3. What do you think God would have to say to you about that fear?

_____

_____

_____

_____

4. How have you previously experienced the discernment that comes from God?

_____

_____

_____

_____

Day 79– Ownership

LETTING GO
OF CONTROL

"Letting go doesn't mean that you don't care about someone anymore. It's just realizing that the only person you really have control over is yourself."

Deborah Reber

"His lord said to him, 'Well done,
good and faithful servant; you were faithful over
a few things, I will make you ruler over many things.
Enter into the joy of your lord.'"

Matthew 25:21 NKJV

When we first start setting boundaries, it can feel like we're putting up fences trying to keep things (or people) out. Boundaries are not about controlling others; they're about taking responsibility for the health and wellbeing of what is ours. Matthew 25:21 tells us that when we are faithful to manage what we've been given, the Lord increases our territory. Learning to set good boundaries is an important step to taking responsibility for managing our relationships and stewarding our inner world.

Setting boundaries is about establishing standards in your life. Someone might want to have a disrespectful conversation with you, but if you've decided you no longer have disrespectful conversations, your boundary might be to ask them to be respectful, and if they are not, to leave the conversation. You're not controlling what the other person is doing, but you're making it clear there are natural consequences to the words and actions they choose. This way, your boundary is not about keeping that person out, but rather about keeping disrespectful conversations out of your life in order to protect your love, joy, hope, and peace. When we get good at setting these kinds of boundaries, we actually protect connection in our lives rather than create disconnection by letting disrespect, fear, and hopelessness in. When you start telling people what you're going to do without telling them what to do, you establish standards for how people can be in a relationship with you.

As with any relational principle, the first person you should practice boundaries with is yourself. We can create boundaries with thoughts and feelings, actions and words. Most of us do not realize we already try to create these boundaries by using shame and unhealthy control that manifests as negative self-talk and self-sabotage. We say things like, "You are so stupid! What is wrong with you? Why would you do that? You're a terrible person." Rebellion is a healthy response to unhealthy control. This is why when we try to use unhealthy control toward ourselves, we do not change, even if we want to. When we realize we have full freedom over our own life, we start to say different things that help us realize the natural consequences to our choices are not what we want. Things like, "You can isolate, but is that helpful? What might be more helpful? You can eat a whole cake, but will that make you feel worse yourself tomorrow? You can yell, but does that ever get you the sustained results you want, or does that just hurt your relationships? What else can you try to get what you really want?" As we get good at realizing we have full freedom, and practice these conversations with ourselves, they will naturally start to spill out toward others.

Prayer

God, thank You for creating me for freedom.
Thank You for my freedom to control myself, and to let others do the same.
Teach me to use empowering language, and create in me a heart to see my spouse, friends, and family behave in an empowered way, too. I choose to banish control from my life and relationships today. Freedom is the way that You lead, and I look to You for Your strength and guidance when I don't feel control in my life. You bring me comfort and peace and extend trust instead of control.

Reflection

1.   When you hear the word "boundaries," what comes to mind?

   _____
   _____
   _____
   _____

2.   Is it primarily a negative, positive, or neutral word to you?
     Why do you think that is?

   _____
   _____
   _____
   _____

3.   In which relationships do you find it most difficult to let go
     of control and let people be free to be themselves?

   _____
   _____
   _____
   _____

4.   Take stock of the emotions you feel daily. Where could you
     establish a boundary to protect love, joy, and peace in your life?

   _____
   _____
   _____
   _____

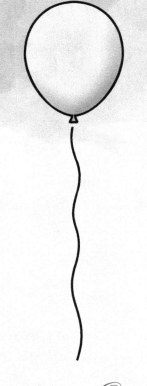

Day 80– Openness

GOD'S JUSTICE

"God's justice is satisfied when there is restoration."

Jessica Nicholas

God's justice doesn't look like human justice. It's so much better! When we set boundaries for ourselves around how we will respond when we or others are scared or hurt, we can step out of the world's idea of justice, which is trial, judgment, and punishment, and instead operate from God's justice, which is repentance, grace, and restoration. Isaiah 30:18 says, "Yet the Lord longs to be gracious to you, therefore He will rise up to show you compassion. For the Lord is a God of justice" (NIV). This tells us that God's grace and compassion are connected to His justice.

We know that fear doesn't bring out the best in us. In fact, some of the worst injustices in the world have come from people fearing others who are different from them. In the same way, some of the greatest expressions of justice have come from people who prayerfully chose their responses in the midst of their fear. We can do the same as we learn to manage our internal world. When fear rises up, we can learn to quiet our thoughts, and connect to God's grace and compassion before we respond. God's justice has one primary goal: relationship! Jesus made a way for love to flow no matter what. His idea of justice is restoration, and that should be our idea of justice, too!

God's idea of justice is so different from ours, often the stories in the Bible seem crazy! Remember how David stole the wife of one of his best warriors, and had that warrior sent to the front line so he could be killed? This was not his finest moment, and murder and adultery are both specifically named in the ten commandments as sin. We can assume that God was not happy about this! And yet, while his behavior had some devastating consequences, God created and communicated boundaries of what was not okay, and his justice also led to the restoration of David's relationship with Him. What's more, God blessed David and Bathsheba's relationship and their son Solomon became the heir to the throne and part of the lineage of Jesus. God's justice is always making a way for full restoration if we are willing to realign our hearts with His. No matter what we've done, there is always a way back into love for us in Jesus, because of His sacrifice for us. As we receive God's justice for ourselves, we get to choose to respond with grace and compassion to others as well.

Prayer

God, thank You for sending Your son so that we could be free from punishment for our sins and mistakes. Your grace and compassion stretch so far beyond our human understanding, and yet it always makes the way for us to stay connected to You and others. Thank You for the restoration of a relationship that is possible through Your justice as I partner with your love.

Reflection

1. How does it impact you to know that God is longing to be gracious to you?

    _____
    _____
    _____
    _____

2. Are there any areas of your life where you are resisting God's grace or restoration, holding yourself to your own sense of justice?

    _____
    _____
    _____
    _____

3. When have you experienced God's justice of restoration in your life?

    _____
    _____
    _____
    _____

4. Does God's justice challenge your understanding of fairness?

    _____
    _____
    _____
    _____

5. Which relationships in your life would you like to start praying for restoration?

    _____
    _____
    _____
    _____

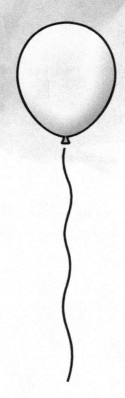

Day 81 – Ownership

WORKING THROUGH UNHEALTHY MINDSETS

"God wants us to let the mind that was in Christ Jesus, that pure, holy, humble mind of Christ, be in us."

Smith Wigglesworth

"For the weapons of our warfare are not carnal but mighty in God for pulling down strongholds, casting down arguments and every high thing that exalts itself against the knowledge of God, bringing every thought into captivity to the obedience of Christ."

2 Corinthians 10:4-5 NKJV

God's goal is not just to transform our hearts, but to transform our minds! Jesus spent much of His ministry helping His disciples and others to align their thinking with the kingdom truth rather than the ways of the world. 2 Corinthians 10:4-5 tells us that the secret to changing our mindsets is to catch our thoughts and bring them into the obedience of Christ. That means that just like we need to have boundaries with people, we need to have boundaries with our thoughts and feelings. We don't just say, "Yes," to a thought because it wanders into our mind, especially if that "yes" means we are saying "no" to the truth. Some thoughts might have no right to be in your mind!

A mindset is a thought that we've made agreements with over and over again, that has become a lens through which we see the world. We then speak, act, and view others through this lens. When we use the same lens, different situations seem to have the same result. If you have a negative lens, you may get negative results, but when you replace your lens with truth, things will start to change. Our mindsets cause repetitive patterns of behavior in our lives. For example, if we have a mindset of rejection, we will go into situations assuming we will be rejected. This will cause us to act fearfully and defensively, keeping our heart behind a metaphorical cement wall. We may interpret a neutral behavior of others as rejection. The people we interact with will sense our fear, and defensiveness, and may interpret it personally, thinking we do not like them, or we are uncaring and do not want to get to know them. They may feel anxious around us. So, guess what? It is true we are more likely to feel "rejected" by those people, but our mindset of fear created our own rejection!

There are countless mindsets that we might need to work through to gain victory in Christ! Mindsets such as selfishness, poverty, rejection, victimhood, superiority, and more. We step into greater levels of freedom when we partner with God by becoming great at recognizing fear-based mindsets, identifying the lies behind them, and replacing these with truth. If we do not believe the new thought right away, that is okay. Like the man whose son needed deliverance in Mark 9:24, we can ask God's help, saying, "I do believe, help my unbelief." It is a life-long process to have the mindsets of Christ, but it is a journey that rewards us richly with abundant life!

---- ✦ ----

Prayer

God, You care not just about my actions, but about my mind and heart.
You know how powerful the mind is to be the birthplace of peace or fear,
defeat or victory. I choose today to break my agreement with unhealthy mindsets
as an act of faith. I choose today not to raise my own mindsets up as idols of truth.
Instead, I hold fast to Your truth about me. As I read Your Word and listen
to Your voice, infuse my heart and mind with Your thoughts.
I submit my thought life to Your Word, knowing that my mindsets
will impact my behavior, and my behavior will affect
the quality of my relationships.

Reflection

. What are some of the "lenses" or mindsets you recognize that God might want to upgrade?

_____

_____

_____

_____

2. How have you been able to recognize wrong mindsets in your life in the past?

_____

_____

_____

_____

3. What strategies have worked for you for transforming your mindsets long-term?

_____

_____

_____

_____

4. How would things change if you recognized your thoughts must be obedient to Christ, who has your best interest in mind?

_____

_____

_____

_____

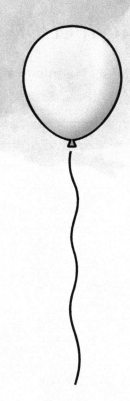

FROM PAIN
TO RESTORATION

"Life is 10% what happens to you and 90% how you react to it."

Charles R. Swindoll

"After you have suffered a little while, the God of all grace, who called you to His eternal glory in Christ, will himself restore you and make you strong, firm, and steadfast."

1 Peter 5:10 NIV

In any relationship, there is opportunity to get hurt. It doesn't matter how perfect someone seems; at some point there will be a disagreement, a misunderstanding, an unmet need or hurt. The goal is that we do not use these as an excuse to disconnect. Instead, we express what we experienced, and take ownership for our hurt. Often, we can feel hurt because someone says or does something that touches on an area of insecurity in us, and so it is important we learn to own what hurt occurred because of our insecurity or assumptions.

Our goal in our relationship is to always check in with the other person, before assuming they meant to hurt us. This, again, requires us to have the ability to have a feeling, notice that feeling, and pause before we react. We then take the step to own our feelings and thoughts and communicate these. For example, "When I saw the look on your face, I felt it might mean I was not good enough." The key is to take ownership for your pain, and your feelings, without blaming the other person for it. "Stop looking at me like I'm not good enough" would be an example of blame and lack of ownership. Life hurts sometimes. It hurts even if there is no one else to blame it on. Sadly, when life hurts, many take it out on the people closest to them, and blame those people for their unhappiness.

When someone comes to you with the goal of proving how hurtful you are, how does it make you feel? Usually not like you want to collaborate, be on their team, or solve problems with them. The goal is to stay on the same team to solve the pain together, and see what can be done to prevent it from happening again. If your teammate accidentally trips you on the field, you don't want to score a goal for the other team to "get back at them." At that point, you're only hurting yourself more. If you cause someone pain and it was intentional, it is important to understand what triggered you to move away from them onto another team, and see what you can take ownership of, so that you are not planting hurt and reaping hurt in return! The goal is to break the cycle of reacting to our pain in ways that cause pain. Instead, choose responses of love that invite both people into restoration and healing. This is how we break the fear of pain and become resilient in relationships.

Prayer

God, You make a way where there is seemingly no way.
You are never at a loss to provide alternatives to disconnection. When I ask,
You are faithful to show me the way of love even in the most difficult circumstances.
I am reminded about how You have protected my connection with You and my heart
by not reacting in pain and anger toward me, instead acting in love.
When I respond rather than react in painful situations,
I not only retain ownership of myself, but give You space
to show me the quickest way through.

Reflection

1. How have you seen the reactions of others impact your relationship and connection with them?

    _____

    _____

    _____

    _____

2. Think of the people closest to you. Do you see them reacting mostly in fight, flight, or freeze?

    _____

    _____

    _____

    _____

3. In the next conflict, how might you better support them by being able to lower their fear? What might they need from you? (You can ask them.)

    _____

    _____

    _____

    _____

4. Evaluate your instinctive reactions to pain. When and how could you step out of your comfort zone and apply the peace and security of God to soothe your pain before reacting?

    _____

    _____

    _____

    _____

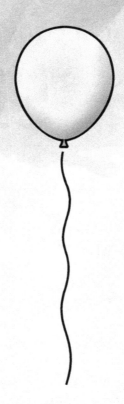

Day 83— Ownership

SETTING
HEALTHY LIMITS

"You need boundaries... Even in our material creations,
boundaries mark the most beautiful of places, between the ocean
and the shore, between the mountains and the plains,
where the canyon meets the river."

William P. Young

*"And just as you want men to do to you,
you also do to them likewise."*

Luke 6:31 NKJV

I've seen many people hurt and in pain because they were exploited time and time again by consumers who kept taking and taking. The only way to change this is to set healthy boundaries and take responsibility for your resources! The more you have cultivated your own resources of love and happiness, the more others are likely to want something from you. We see in the life of Jesus that it wasn't until people started to see His wisdom and power that they started to gather around Him to receive some of what He had. Jesus, however, never let the needs of others decide what He would give. He managed His own resources, time, and energy, and in so doing protected His ability to give at all. We can do the same!

Your boundaries can help protect you against pain in a healthy way. When we fail to set good limits with "consumers," we end up feeling exploited, and being exploited is painful. It causes us to be tempted to live like a victim. When we're great at setting limits on our time and resources, we can avoid this kind of pain. Luke 6:31 says, "And just as you want men to do to you, you also do to them likewise." The obvious way to interpret this is to treat people the way you want to be treated. But what this verse also means is that you should not allow people to treat you in ways that violate your priorities and get in the way of love. Setting limits can be the most loving thing we do! In fact, Ally has worked with many people who were upset that their parents did not have boundaries and limits for them, because they never had to practice self-control or ownership.

Consumers approach relationships from the viewpoint of only what they can get. They see something attractive, like happiness, and instead of cultivating happiness themselves they try to consume all of somebody else's happiness. If we and others are great at setting limits on this behavior and don't automatically jump into "rescue" mode, we actually communicate to the other person, "I love you, and I fully trust that as I set this limit, you'll remember who you are and who your source is!" This gives them the opportunity to snap out of their consumer behavior and make proactive choices again. What a gift! If we don't set boundaries with consumers, we feel used and exploited, and this can lead to offense, bitterness, and resentment that destroys a relationship. When we set boundaries, we're able to protect and share our resources effectively and avoid the pain of disconnection.

Prayer

God, where pain has been scary in the past, I now trust You to hold my hand and walk me through it. Thank You that while there may be a battle between fear and love in my life, love will win as I partner with you. I refuse to let pain dictate my openness to love. Show me how to set the best limits in my life, relationships, and actions. I want to have the right balance just as You would have limits to what You extend based on what people need, want, and desire. Enlarge my discernment in this season and forever so I can measure the best balance in each area of my life.

Reflection

1. What are the situations that cause you to feel exhausted or burnt out at the end of the day?

   _____

   _____

   _____

   _____

2. Are there any beautiful things that come to mind when you think of times where you have seen healthy boundaries?

   _____

   _____

   _____

   _____

3. When you feel burnt out and stretched, how does this impact your life, mood, and relationships?

   _____

   _____

   _____

   _____

4. How might setting boundaries with people or situations allow you to be a better representation of Christ with your mood, energy, and life?

   _____

   _____

   _____

   _____

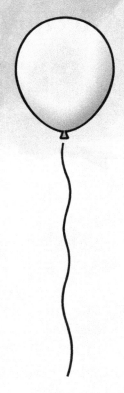

LETTING DOWN YOUR ARMOR

"David knew that it wasn't in the armor that he found his strength, but in his God. This is how he could run to the battlefront— the battle was already won."

Che Ahn

> *"As a fair exchange—I speak as to my children—*
> *open wide your hearts also."*
>
> 2 Corinthians 6:13 NIV

God knows that the only way to a full heart is to first open it up to be filled. 2 Corinthians 6:13 challenges us to open our hearts wide! Of course, this can be scary, as a wide-open heart is also vulnerable to pain. If we let our fear of pain get too big, our instinct can be to put armor around our heart in an effort to self-protect. We might keep it safe from pain, but we also leave no space to let love in! Instead, when we choose to let God be the protector of our hearts, we can let down our armor and open ourselves up to real love.

When we do not have healthy boundaries, we put up walls to keep pain out. The walls are an attempt to stay safe, but the tragedy of this is that the armor we think is keeping us safe is also preventing us from having relationships. Self-protection doesn't help us to become healthy; it only keeps us from facing our fears. If we confuse armor with healthy boundaries, we will succeed in keeping love out, rather than protecting it. Boundaries that set limits enable love to flourish and cultivate connection and intimacy. The goal of good boundaries is to offer your whole heart to create strong, lasting relationships.

When we own our own heart, we are diligent to allow it to receive the love of God, and have healthy self-love, then in turn, to receive the love of others. Getting in the way of God's love for you and saying you know you are unlovable is not godly. Having healthy love for yourself is humility. Disliking yourself and putting yourself down does not honor

God! When we learn a healthy love and respect for ourselves, and give that to ourselves, we start to feel we are strong enough to not need armor to protect us. We realize no weapon formed against us will prosper! We are wrapped in an entire fortress of God's love around our heart. Psalm 144:2 says, "He is my loving God and my fortress, my stronghold and my deliverer, my shield, in whom I take refuge..." We alone have the power to let people in or kick them out of that sacred place God has created for our heart to flourish. We do not have to live in fear of what others do, because we trust what we will do.

Prayer

God, thank You for creating me for love.
Where I've put up armor to protect my own heart, I now release it back into Your care.
I know that armor doesn't just keep pain out; it keeps love out as well.
I choose to take down my armor and be open to love today.
In each and every conversation I have the power to dwell inside a fortress of your love.
Show me how You love my friends so I can partner with that approach.
I want to be defenseless with the people You have given me,
because love should lead and You will protect me.
Thank You, Lord, for modeling a life that is open and vulnerable
without armor and swords.

Reflection

Describe a situation in which you noticed a protective boundary being so high it caused some harm.

_____

_____

_____

_____

. Are there boundaries you have built self-protectively that might prevent you from intimacy and love?

_____

_____

_____

_____

. When have you been able to resist the temptation to retreat from relationships or to put up protective armor?

_____

_____

_____

_____

. Our spiritual calling is to love and be loved by God and people. What choices could you make to grow in love?

_____

_____

_____

_____

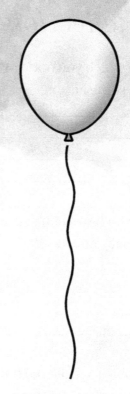

Day 85~ Ownership

FROM REJECTED TO ACCEPTED

"So many of us have believed that we need to labor and perform for God so that we can gain an identity, so that we might be accepted. But in the Kingdom, we start off accepted."

Beni Johnson The Happy

"For you did not receive the spirit of bondage again to fear, but you received the Spirit of adoption by whom we cry out, 'Abba, Father.'"

Romans 8:15 NKJV

In John 4, when Jesus meets the woman at the well, she is the picture of rejection. He tells her that she has been married five times, and the man she is now with is not even her husband. The woman must have felt rejected to her core, and yet meeting Jesus changed everything. He broke all the local customs by taking the time to talk to her, to demonstrate his acceptance for her and to give her the very thing that could heal her when no man could. "Everyone who drinks this water will be thirsty again, but whoever drinks the water I give them will never thirst. Indeed, the water I give them will become in them a spring of water welling up to eternal life" (John 4:13-14). This woman left this encounter with Jesus changed, and became an evangelist in her city. Rejection doesn't define us when we stay close to the Father!

We are completely loved and accepted in God, but that doesn't mean rejection from people doesn't hurt when it happens. When we stay connected to the Father and allow the Holy Spirit to bring healing to our hearts, we can overcome rejection without letting it change how we choose to love. Other people's choices can hurt, but as sons and daughters of God, we can choose to retain ownership of ourselves in the midst of pain, to keep our hearts open and to remain strong as we overcome rejection. Romans 8:15 says, "For you did not receive the spirit of bondage again to fear, but you received the Spirit of adoption by whom we cry out, 'Abba, Father.'" We overcome rejection when we keep our identity rooted in our Father in heaven who accepts us no matter what.

While it's important that we learn to love each other well, our primary source of unconditional love and acceptance will always be the Father. People will let you down, but He never will! He is the ultimate source of love and the one we can draw on when we're in pain. There is no perfect relationship outside of a relationship with God, and therefore we will all experience relational pain from time to time. We stay open to the option to be healthy during these times of pain by choosing not to let the pain, the rejection, or the betrayal define us, but let God the Father define us instead. He is the place to go for validation, for identity, and for healing. To overcome rejection, you may need to confront orphan beliefs. Orphan beliefs come up when our needs haven't been met for a long time. When we receive the Father's love, it confronts and breaks down these orphan beliefs and restores our trust!

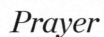

Prayer

God, thank You that in You I am accepted, not rejected. Thank You that any rejection I've experienced in the past doesn't change my identity as chosen in Your kingdom. Where I've let rejection set my course, I now choose to let Your acceptance lead me into love instead. I promise to lead with acceptance just as you do, Jesus. I will open my arms of acceptance for my relationships. You were rejected many, many times, yet You come to me with acceptance. How wonderful are You, God? Thank You for being so accepting of me. Show me how to be so accepting to others.

Reflection

1. In what ways does the fear of rejection impact your current or potential relationships?

   _____

   _____

   _____

   _____

2. How has your identity as a fully accepted child of God impacted how you view rejection?

   _____

   _____

   _____

   _____

3. What is the price you are paying when you operate out of fear of rejection? What are the pros and cons of fearing rejection?

   _____

   _____

   _____

   _____

4. What would you need from God or yourself in order to change your feelings of rejection?

   _____

   _____

   _____

   _____

Day 86 – Openness

UPGRADING YOUR RELATIONAL SKILL SET

"The key to happiness is really progress and growth and constantly working on yourself and developing something."

Lewis Howes

"Enlarge the place of your tent, And let them stretch out the curtains of your dwellings; Do not spare; Lengthen your cords, And strengthen your stakes. For you shall expand to the right and to the left."

Isaiah 54:2-4 NKJV

No matter what relational skills or boundaries we've learned over the years, we always have the opportunity to develop better ones! I know people who wrongly use boundaries as a self-protection tool. They put up walls and withhold themselves from others, thinking they're using good boundaries. This doesn't work! If our boundaries are serving the goal of independence, we've got them all wrong. Boundaries are designed to help us manage our resources so we can keep loving and share our lives with people. Boundaries are essentially about taking care of yourself. If your motivation is to sustain love, generosity, and fruitfulness, you will set boundaries that keep you nourished and connected to others. If your motivation is to self-protect, you will cause problems in your relationship and remain distant from others. Invest in learning all there is to know about what you need to nourish and stay connected.

Taking responsibility for our lives and learning to control ourselves and not other people is a lifetime journey of exchanging old skills for better ones. When we decide to be loving and unselfish, we take the time and effort to learn the very best skills we can so that we produce great fruit in our own lives and also have something valuable to give others. Isn't it empowering to know that you can learn the skills of healthy boundaries? As you share your life with others you can intentionally develop the skills to protect and sustain what's important to you. Isaiah 54:2-5 encourages us to "enlarge the place of your tent...for you shall expand to the right and to the left." This tells us that increase is part of God's kingdom. He is always inviting you to take new ground!

Jesus set boundaries in His life all the time. In Luke 8, Jesus raises Jairus's daughter from the dead. Jesus is in the midst of a crowd of people who want healing. Some of them may have been waiting a long time or in severe pain or need, but Jesus says, "Yes," to Jairus, and therefore "no" to everyone else. We know that if Jesus wanted to self-protect and keep people out, He could have simply left. He didn't use His boundaries to distance from the crowd; He used them to protect His priority of obeying what the Father asked Him to do. His motivation was to sustain love, generosity, and fruitfulness, and so He learned to say "yes" and "no." He demonstrated and practiced skills that kept His relationships in a place of health.

Prayer

God, thank You for always giving me the opportunity for an upgrade.
It is not my heart to set boundaries that hinder me. It is not my goal to set boundaries
that limit You or Your plan for my life. I choose to recognize that I am the person who
chooses my boundaries, and I will no longer act as a victim to others.
Help me to respect my own boundaries and the boundaries of others with love.
Thank You for the abundant opportunities to learn to manage my own resources well.
I commit to learning how to protect and cultivate love in my life. Reveal to me
where I can practice the new skills I am learning today!

Reflection

When you look at the boundaries you have set, are they serving
their purpose of helping to take care of you?

_____

_____

_____

_____

2. Which of your boundaries are motivated by self-love vs.
self-protection?

_____

_____

_____

_____

3. How do your boundaries help you manage your resources so
you can keep loving and sharing your life with people?

_____

_____

_____

_____

4. How might you re-establish or upgrade your boundaries today?

_____

_____

_____

_____

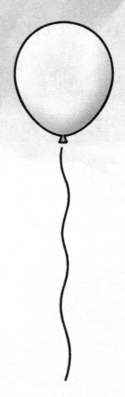

Day 87 – Ownership

THE POWER OF SELF-CONTROL

*"There is no greatness apart from self-control.
Development that does not include self-government will only
guarantee our mediocrity."*

Graham Cooke

> *"Whoever has no rule over his own spirit Is like a city broken down, without walls."*
>
> Proverbs 25:28 NKJV

When two people in a relationship show each other that they can control themselves on a regular basis, trust is built. They don't have to keep wondering if the other person will do what they say; they know they will! If someone gets it wrong from time to time, the trust is strong enough to overcome the mistake. The same is true for ourselves. When we consistently show ourselves that we follow through with what we have said we'll do, we build trust in our own ability to reach goals, accomplish tasks, and follow through with commitments. This builds self-confidence and an overcoming lifestyle. We can all start by setting small, manageable goals, and slowly increasing until we feel the momentum that self-control creates in our lives.

How good are you at setting boundaries with yourself? Self-control is at the core of having ownership. It means that you can tell yourself what to do, and trust yourself to follow through with it. Sounds simple, but most of us know this can be one of the hardest things to master. Once you learn it, it impacts every area of your life. Proverbs 25:28 says, "Whoever has no rule over his own spirit Is like a city broken down, without walls." This tells us that when we haven't learned self-control, we are likely to experience chaos in our lives. We can all learn to establish and keep boundaries with ourselves, and become great at directing our lives toward our goals.

To practice self-control requires a goal. If your goal is a healthy body, it will take self-control to eat healthy and go to the gym. If your goal is to write a book, it will take self-control to sit down every day and write. Learning to follow through with what we've told ourselves we will do is the only way to achieve our goals, and the only way to become a responsible person. The goal is the thing we're saying "yes" to, and it defines the "no's" that will be required as a result. This is what it looks like to set boundaries with yourself; it's as simple as choosing the "yes" and aligning your life with it. This only works if the goal is entirely your own. As soon as someone else is setting your goals, you're no longer controlling yourself, but letting someone else control you.

Prayer

God, thank You that self-control allows me to manage the increasing levels of freedom You have for me. Thank You that as I make choices, follow through with actions, and react, rather than respond in situations, I make myself available for increase. You have given so many gifts to the world and one of the most important gifts that You have given us is self-control. Thank You that You not only have given us this gift, but You instruct us in how to grow in it and use it properly. Thank You, God, that Self-control places the responsibility back in our hands to manage our lives. We are delighted to be in charge of our lives and grow in this gift.

Reflection

What are the thoughts and feelings that come to mind when you think about self-control?

_____

_____

_____

_____

What are some of the gifts self-control might have to offer you?

_____

_____

_____

_____

What could exercising self-control in relationships give you?

_____

_____

_____

_____

What is one small but realistic step you can take to increase your relational self-control today?

_____

_____

_____

_____

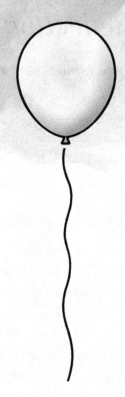

Day 88– Openness

BUILDING AN ENVIRONMENT OF LOVE

*"We've got this gift of love, but love is like a precious plant.
You can't just accept it and leave it in the cupboard or just think it's
going to get on by itself. You've got to keep watering it.
You've got to really look after it and nurture it."*

John Lennon

"If the home is deserving, let your peace rest on it;
if it is not, let your peace return to you."

he atmosphere of peace is the reward for our labor, and it is the flourishing of divine order, divine health, and divine prosperity in our lives. When we do the work, every part of our lives will be nourished, growing and thriving. We are owners in the environments we set for ourselves. It takes a lot of work to build an environment of love and connection, but once it is built it is much easier to maintain.

The limits we set in our lives and close relationships are all about creating an environment of love, which is the environment that human beings thrive in! When we lay a firm foundation of unconditional love and acceptance with others, we've created the foundation for this environment. An environment of perfect peace, wellbeing, and wholeness. In Matthew 10:13, Jesus sends out His disciples. He gives them instructions for entering a house: "If the home is deserving, let your peace rest on it; if it is not, let your peace return to you." Because of the Holy Spirit living in us, each of us can create within ourselves an environment of peace that impacts every room we walk into. When we work at cultivating this with others, our marriages, friendships, and other relationships become places of peace too.

An environment of love is cultivated when we've actively built the pillars of love, honor, self-control, responsibility, truth, faith, and vision in our relationships, and raised a structure that protects these pillars. Our boundaries are part of this process. As we practice choosing to cultivate our own resources and share them with others in a way that protects our priorities, we're building these pillars brick by brick. This is what makes fighting for connection worth it! As we practice, we get so good at protecting connections that we start to live in the fruits of our labor! We've talked a lot about the hard work that is needed to reset your mindsets, but let's not forget that the hard work leads to the end goal of an environment of love. Don't let go of your vision today! Keep establishing new habits in your life until an environment of love is your reality.

Prayer

God, You created people to flourish in an environment of love.
As I reflect on this wisdom, I see new options for my relational goals
and needs to be met. I see that I have Your power to love in me,
and that by choosing to create an environment of love, I benefit from that love!
As I choose to love in my communication and boundaries,
I cultivate an environment around me in which people feel valued,
safe, nourished, protected, and understood. Thank You for entrusting me
with this power and gift to bring out the best in others and myself.

Reflection

1. Practically, what could an environment of love look like in your home?

   _____

   _____

   _____

   _____

2. What are the building blocks for creating an environment of love? What gets to stay, and what will need to go?

   _____

   _____

   _____

   _____

3. What one thing could you do to move toward creating an atmosphere of love in your home today?

   _____

   _____

   _____

   _____

4. What conversations will you need to have to facilitate this?

   _____

   _____

   _____

   _____

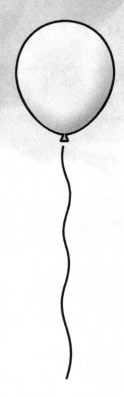

Day 89 – Ownership

LIVING AN EMPOWERED LIFE

"Bad emotions are not going to go away just by praying longer and harder and fasting. We replace them by repenting of wrong core beliefs that hinder confidence in the power of our prayers."

Steve Backlund

"Repent, then, and turn to God, so that your sins may be wiped out, that times of refreshing may come from the Lord."

Acts 3:19 NIV

You are the owner of your life! Picture the garden of your life and the tools you have to cultivate it into a place of flourishing relationships. You have the power to uproot thoughts and language, and make the choice to repent from these and choose new thoughts and language. Acts 3:19 says, "Repent, then, and turn to God, so that your sins may be wiped out, that times of refreshing may come from the Lord." Repentance is the first step to refreshing! God celebrates every time we turn from wrong thinking and align ourselves with the truth of who He is and who we are in Him.

Repentance simply means to change the way you think. Becoming perfected in love often requires a lot of changing our mind as we let go of our old habits and renew our mind. What are you thinking that isn't true? These thoughts could be "I'm not valuable" or "I'll never find love." On this journey of perfecting our own process, we need to get really good at distinguishing lies from truth! When the thought "I'm not valuable" (or any other) pops up, we don't have to agree with it. Instead, we should repent of believing the lie that we're not valuable and ask the Holy Spirit for the truth instead. We know our value is determined by what someone was willing to pay for us, and since Jesus gave His life, we know we are valued! When we choose to agree with the truth, we're agreeing with God's kingdom and choosing an empowered mindset. Keep doing this for every individual lie that comes up until they're all dealt with!

Being open to love is the most rewarding choice you could ever make! I have seen scores of people change their lives and open themselves up to love by choosing empowered thinking over disempowered thinking. Jesus told us that our priority on this earth is to learn to love. Imagine we all got really, really good at this! Start today by renouncing the lies you've been believing and replacing them with truth. With every new truth, you're building the life of love God intended for you to have, built on His unconditional love.

Prayer

God, thank You for the authority You have given me.
I choose to renounce every lie that separates me from my true identity in Christ.
If there are specific lies I'm believing, please highlight them now. I break all agreeme
with these lies in Jesus's name and replace them with truth today. I stand in You, Jes
ready to live a life that brings hope, harmony, and happiness to myself and those th
you have given to me. I delight in the day where I am connected to You
and I can extend Your love and joy to the rest of the world.
You empower me to live out the fullness of my purpose
and destiny! Thank You, Jesus.

Reflection

1. What disempowering thoughts or language have you used this week, and how might you replace those with empowered thoughts and language?

   _____

   _____

   _____

   _____

2. What would it look like and feel like to have a time of refreshing from God after turning away from old thoughts?

   _____

   _____

   _____

   _____

3. How would your relationships be impacted for the better if you continued on the journey of continuing to love?

   _____

   _____

   _____

   _____

4. What thoughts, feelings, and decisions would change if you aligned your life with the primary goal of learning to love?

   _____

   _____

   _____

   _____

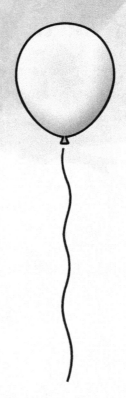

LIVING A LIFE
OF FRUITFULNESS

*"If you don't like what you are reaping, you had better change
what you have been sowing."*

Jim Rohn

Reflection

Are there times you say or do things that are devaluing to yourself?

_____

_____

_____

_____

What heart-level change might you need to make that will produce
the visible fruit of changing your language and actions?

_____

_____

_____

_____

Describe a relationship or situation you are in where you are
waiting for someone else to change in order to feel settled,
peaceful, or happy.

_____

_____

_____

_____

What might you do differently to initiate the change you are
hoping for?

_____

_____

_____

_____

For More from Jeremy & Dr. Ally Butrous
please visit Radiantthoughts.com

CPSIA information can be obtained
at www.ICGtesting.com
Printed in the USA
LVHW030519200821
695646LV00002B/304

I magine a man who doesn't value himself gets into a new relationship. While the couple are in the "honeymoon period," everything seems wonderful. They both have every reason to believe that the relationship will be one full of honor and mutual respect. The first time she yells at him, he brushes it off because she was stressed out. The second time, he yells back, and before long, disrespectful communication becomes a pattern in their relationship. One day, he realizes he wants things to change. When one person decides they no longer want disrespectful conversations, they must be open to creating something new. Now, he has an opportunity to value himself enough to learn how to act valuable in a conflict. Next time a disrespectful conversation happens, he refuses to participate in it.

Changing your relational pattern is all about identifying what isn't working and finding new strategies to shift things around so they do start working! Every choice you make has an effect on the people around you. If your choices are making a mess, good news! New choices will create new results in your life. Proverbs 23:7 says, "For as he thinks in his heart, so is he." Change begins in our heart when we decide to take responsibility for our choices and live fruitful lives.

It should be good news to us that setting up new patterns in our lives starts in our own hearts, and is worked out in our own choices. It doesn't depend on what anybody else does or doesn't do! We all have the power to be open to change in our lives. Powerlessness, irresponsibility, and lack of boundaries in relationships are signs that we're not valuing our lives as God does. When these things are going on in our heart, the effects include unhealthy triangulation patterns, unfruitful communication, and unfulfilled relationships. On the other hand, honoring God's value for your life will have a different effect on your life. It will challenge you to set limits in every area of your life. Setting healthy limits in our lives is honoring our value. Every time we say, "Yes," to something, we are saying "no" to everything else.

Prayer

God, I ask that You would search my heart and know me today.
I want my heart to be clean, healthy, and pleasing to you.
Thank You that as I position my heart toward You,
I begin to manifest new behaviors that cultivate healthy connection.
You are the fruitful vine that brings forth the best fruit.
Guide me into a life that displays fruitfulness from my connection to Your heart.
I love You, Jesus, and love to live my life according to the pattern
that You have shown me in Jesus.
You are the best!